Putting on a Play

BY SUSAN AND STEPHEN JUDY

Gifts of Writing: Creative Projects with Words and Art
The English Teacher's Handbook
An Introduction to Teaching Writing
The ABCs of Literacy (Stephen Judy)
Writing in Reality (Stephen Judy)

Susan and Stephen Judy

Putting on a Play

A Guide to Writing and Producing Neighborhood Drama

Charles Scribner's Sons / New York

For Michael John Judy,
born playmaker.

Copyright © 1982 Susan and Stephen Judy

Library of Congress Cataloging in Publication Data
Judy, Susan J.   Putting on a play.
   Includes index.
   Summary: Discusses ways to develop your
imagination, transform your ideas into different
kinds of plays, and present your finished
product to an audience
   1. Children's plays—Presentation, etc.—
Juvenile literature. 2. Playwriting—Juvenile
literature. 3. Theater—Production and
direction—Juvenile literature. [1. Plays—
Production and direction. 2. Playwriting]
I. Judy, Stephen N. II. Title.
PN3157.J8   792'.0226   82-3179
ISBN 0-684-17452-9   AACR2

1 3 5 7 9 11 13 15 17 19   F/C   20 18 16 14 12 10 8 6 4 2

Printed in the United States of America

Contents

Introduction

Just about everybody likes to make a play. From the time babies can walk and talk, they enjoy playing "let's pretend," dressing up in costumes, and wearing makeup. When we—the authors of this book—were young, "Cowboys and Indians" was a game we played for hours, and we see young people nowadays having the same kind of fun playing "Space Heroes and Aliens." We put on skits and plays when we were in the Scouts, and it interests us to see some of the same gags and stunts being used in the Scout troops that our own children belong to. Just about everybody likes to make a play.

We suppose one reason you are reading this book is that you already have had some experience with plays. We'll bet that at one time or another you have gathered your family together to watch a show you have carefully rehearsed: a skit or dance or pantomime or puppet play or magic show. You may have even forced a family pet into playing a role for you, making a good-tempered cat or dog be a bear in a cave or a lion in a circus. You know, then, that the most important ingredient of a successful play is *not* a stage or costumes or even live animals, but *imagination*. In playmaking, you can pretend to be anything or anybody you want to be, and you can cast a spell over your audience so they believe in what you have become.

This book is no substitute for your imagination. We can't tell you exactly how to make a play or what characters to invent. We can't decide what costumes your characters should wear (or whether you will need costumes at all). But over the years, as we have worked with young people in school and in neighborhood theater classes, we have come up with a number of ideas for playmaking. The purpose of this book is to share those ideas with you, helping you make your plays even more imaginative and successful than they already are.

We will suggest some ideas for plays that you may not have tried before, such as:

• plays without words (sometimes called mime or pantomime), where the actor or actress must get across the characters and ideas simply by using gestures and facial expressions.

• "radio" plays made on a tape recorder, complete with sound effects, that can be played for audiences later or maybe even broadcast over a local radio station.

• reader's theater, in which actors and actresses don't actually "perform" or memorize lines, but read something—a short story, a play, a series of poems, even their own writing—and bring it alive for an audience.

• screen plays written to be made into a movie or recorded on videotape.

We will also share some ideas about the production of plays, including:

• how to create a stage in your living room or backyard using a bedsheet and a clothesline.

• how to advertise your play around the neighborhood so you will have a good audience.

• how to calm the nerves of your lead actor or actress when he or she comes down with the first-night jitters. We'll even offer some suggestions on how you can "take the show on the road," entertaining audiences outside your neighborhood in places like schools and libraries.

This is a book that you don't need to read cover to cover. Since you'll want to try out different ideas at different times, it might be a good idea to flip through the book right now to see which of the ideas appeal to you most. This book can also be shared with friends, other people who might like to put on plays with you. We hope that the ideas in the book will excite you enough that you may even want to form a theater company or drama club that writes and presents plays regularly.

Sometimes we will use a term from the theater that may not be familiar to you. Whenever this happens, we'll explain what it means, but we will also define and describe it in a glossary at the back of the book. Whenever you see a word in **boldface type,** you can check it in the glossary if you need to.

At the beginning of a baseball game, the umpire gets things started by saying, PLAY BALL! We'll start off this book by simply saying that you should go out and do what the book is all about:

PLAY!

Part I

Playmaking

chapter 1

Warm-ups: Preparing Yourself as an Actor or Actress

Although you may not be consciously aware of it, you have been acting all your life. First, as people, all of us play roles. With your teachers you might be your serious self or your studious self; with your parents you might be your helpful self or your argumentative self or your relaxed self; with your friends you might play your crazy or silly role; with younger brothers and sisters you may play the role of the advisor or the boss. The way you talk, your gestures and facial expressions, and your body language depend on your "audience."

In addition, playing "let's pretend" is a part of growing up. As a very small child, you probably learned to say what a doggy and a kitty and a cow say. You probably pretended you were a mother, a doctor, an astronaut, a famous singer. You might have acted out your favorite storybook, TV, or movie character—Peter Pan, Cinderella, Superman, Luke Skywalker, or Christopher Robin. In your daydreams, you've probably thought about what it would be like to be a player on a pro football team, a reporter on national television, a ballet dancer in *Swan Lake,* a space pilot in orbit around Saturn, a private detective or a policeman solving a big crime.

Pretending to be someone else lets you try out the various parts of your personality. It also lets you express different ideas and emotions and become, for a time, someone or something else. The purpose of this chapter is to help you extend and develop some of the skills you've already developed as an actor or actress.

Using Your Body

Acting skills involve both the use of your body and your voice. The first activities in this chapter are intended to help you become more flexible in the use of your body. One of the best ways to relax your body and to practice becoming free with your body is to move to music. This is an activity that you can do alone or with a group of friends. Classical music provides a variety of moods that suggest different kinds of movement. As you listen to the music, try to become aware of each part of your body and make that part of your body respond to the rhythm and the feeling of the music. Start with your head. Let it move from side to side and back and forth. Let your eyes and nose and mouth and cheeks respond to the music. Move your ears, if you can. Let your neck and shoulders into the act; then move your arms, elbows, wrists, hands, and fingers. Move at the waist, hips, and knees. Finally let your feet and toes respond to the music. Try to keep your whole body moving to the music at the same time for a while; then focus again on different parts of your body, moving them in as many ways as you can think of. Feel the flexibility of each part and explore what each part can do. Play both fast music and slow music, dramatic music and peaceful music.

The following are good selections of music for movement:

Debussy, *La Mer*
Stravinsky, *Firebird Suite*

Saint-Saëns, *Carnival of the Animals*
Strauss, *2001: Space Odyssey*
Moussorgsky, *Pictures at an Exhibition*
Grieg, *Peer Gynt Suite*
Tchaikovsky, *The Nutcracker Suite* or *Sleeping Beauty*
Wagner, *Ride of the Valkyries*
Bach, *Fugue No. 2 in C Minor*

Try doing your movement to music in front of a mirror to see all the ways in which your body can move, or dance in front of a blank wall with a bright light shining behind you. Use your body to make shapes on the wall. If you are working with a friend, make "shadow sculptures" together.

Play Ball. This activity is one that you can do alone or with others. Begin by imagining that you are holding a beach ball. How big is it? How soft or firm is it? Feel its texture. Imagine its weight. Now toss it up in the air and catch it. Toss it higher and higher each time. Toss it and let it drop to the ground. Does it bounce? If you are playing with someone else, play catch with the beach ball. First throw it gently and then throw it hard. Keep in mind its weight and size as you play with it.

Now imagine you have a baseball. How is its weight and texture and size different from the beach ball? Toss it up. Try to hit the ceiling with it. Play catch with it. Then imagine a tennis ball. Bounce it on the floor; toss it in the air; bounce it under your legs. Pretend you have three tennis balls and try to juggle them. Now juggle Ping-Pong balls. Bounce the Ping-Pong ball on the floor, on the ceiling, under your legs. Keep in mind the size and weight and texture of the balls as you play with them.

Fire. You are a stack of brush lying in a heap on the ground. It's a dry August day. Try to arrange your body in a pile. Feel the dryness in your limbs. Suddenly, someone throws a lighted match on you. It begins to kindle in one of your parts. Part by part, your body begins to crackle and flame. Gradually make each part of your body crackle and flame until you become a huge fire rising higher and higher in the sky. Make the parts of your body dance like flames and jump like sparks as you become a raging fire. Use every part of your body to express the movement of the blaze. Now it begins to rain; it begins gradually, a drop at a time. Feel each drop as it falls into the flame and sizzles. As the rain falls harder the fire begins to die, gradually becoming smaller and smaller and losing its energy. Soon there are just a few small flames trying to reach up. They too become smaller and smaller until the fire is finally out. A few ashes and coals remain motionless on the ground.

As you do this activity, try to involve all of your body—your eyes and mouth, your arms and legs, your fingers and toes. Let your body be flexible in moving up and down, out and in. Feel the heat, the flame, the water, the coolness as it affects each part of you.

Marionettes. You are a wooden puppet with strings attached to your head, shoulders, elbows, wrists, knees, and feet. You have been left in a heap on the floor. Your body is a tangled mess. All at once, someone pulls the control to which your strings are attached and jerks you to your feet. But the strings are still tangled and your hands and legs are crossed up. Then, the puppeteer picks up a wrist string and untangles one wrist; she does the same with the knee string. As the puppeteer puts you through various actions, feel the pull of the string at your elbows and knees, at your wrists and feet. Feel the string holding your head upright. First the puppeteer makes you march. Feel the strings lifting each knee. The puppeteer loves marching and she makes the knees come higher and higher each time she marches you around the room. Next, she makes you do a silly dance by jiggling the strings and making your hands and feet flop around uncontrollably. Then she makes you become a ballet dancer moving gracefully to slow music—turning, leaping, and gliding. Next she has you play hopscotch. Now pretend that the puppeteer's little brother has gotten hold of you. He doesn't know how to work marionettes, and he pulls the strings in a jerky and unpredictable way, dropping your head, yanking on a knee and elbow, pulling your feet up too fast.

Keep in mind, as you play the part of a puppet, that you have strings attached to various parts of your body. Feel the strings as they are pulled, and let the part that has the string attached lead the rest of your body. If you are working with others, take turns playing the part of the puppeteer, who calls out what strings are being pulled and how they are being pulled—gently, quickly, jerkily, etc.

Mirror Images. This is an activity done in pairs. Stand facing your partner. One of you is the leader, and the other mirrors the leader's actions. The leader should begin slowly with simple actions, and the follower should be very precise in the imitations. Gradually involve more parts of your body and make your actions more complicated. Try speeding up your movements and see if the follower is still able to imitate them exactly. After one person has been the leader, switch and let the follower create the actions. You may want to try this to music. Again, try to incorporate all of your body into the activity.

Sounders and Movers. This activity requires at least two participants, and may be done in fairly large groups. One group (or person) acts as the sounders and their job is to create a rhythmic sound. They may do this by clapping, patting parts of their bodies (like knees), tapping or stomping their feet, or combining all of those. Or, they may use "instruments": a wooden spoon on a pan or pan lid, two spoons or pencils, two blocks or chunks of wood, two jar lids, etc. First, the sounders get together and create a rhythm. They may do this in unison, or they may let each person contribute a part to the rhythm. The rhythm should last just a few seconds and be repeated over and over; you will want to make the beats vary in length and in loudness. CLAP clap CLAP clap/tap tappity tap tap/CLAP CLAP CLAP.

After the sounders have established their rhythm, the movers move to the rhythm. They may decide as a group what movements they will match to the sound; or one person may act as a leader with the others following; or each person may create his own actions to the rhythm. Again, try to get as many parts of your body as possible moving. Then, let the sounders become the movers and the movers become the sounders.

The Machine. As a group, create a candy-making machine, a sock mender, or a spider catcher. One person starts an action which is repeated over and over, for example, swinging her arms back and forth. A second person adds an action coordinating with the first person, in this case, perhaps lying on his back and kicking his feet up each time the arms swing toward him. Then a third person adds an action coordinated with one part of the machine, and so on, until each person has become a part. In addition, each person may want to create a sound to match his or her movement: a buzz, a click, splat, or hum. You might make a rule that no one can use a part of the body that has already been used; that way you'll get some unique actions.

Feelings. In this activity, you use facial expressions, gesture, and posture to express different emotions. You may like to practice trying to communicate attitudes and feelings in front of a mirror. With a group, you can turn this into a game. Have members of the group take turns acting out an emotion; the rest of the group guesses what the actor is trying to communicate. Here are some you might like to try:

happy	excited
angry	proud
fearful	nervous
sorry	jealous
bored	amused
sad	shocked

Other Body Warm-ups. Work on developing both flexibility and control with your body by becoming . . .

- a piece of ice melting on the sidewalk.
- a leaf in the wind.
- a piece of clothing on the clothesline on a windy day.
- a piece of clothing in the dryer.

- popcorn being popped.
- a plant pushing through the ground and reaching toward the sun.

Observation

When you act, you become someone other than yourself, someone who may like different foods and pastimes, hold different beliefs, think different thoughts, dream different dreams. People's thoughts and feelings are often manifested in their behavior. Some people are more nervous than others; some more serious, more relaxed, friendlier, sillier, crabbier, slower, or faster. A skill that will help you improve your ability to be someone else is *observation*. Good actors learn to observe others and perfect the precise mannerisms that project a sense of a character as a total and *real* person. They don't just say lines dramatically, but they move in such a way that the character comes alive.

In order to learn more about people's behavior and mannerisms, spend some time watching them to see what they do. Observe their gestures, their facial expressions, the way they use their hands, the way they walk, how they hold their heads, how they stand. Notice their reactions to the events around them. You may be unconsciously aware of many mannerisms and reactions of friends, teachers, and members of your family, but watch them more closely to heighten your awareness of how they do things, of how they express emotion.

Observe people in public places. Watch how they greet other people, laugh, respond to animals, comb their hair. Notice what different people do when they pass mirrors or big glass windows. Do they stare at themselves, sneak a peek, or ignore the image? What do people do when confronted by a puddle? How is a mother's response different from a child's? How do different people handle an unexpected sneeze or burp? Look at people chewing gum or their nails, reading the paper, cleaning their glasses, tying their shoelaces. Look at people's habits at the dinner table. Watch their reactions to a surprise rainstorm.

After you have watched, try out some of the characteristics and mannerisms you've discovered. You might want to practice in front of a mirror or with a friend and work to refine your imitations. (Note: Sometimes unique mannerisms can be identified as a particular person's. Make sure your imitations are done in private, or in such a way that no one feels he/she is being teased or mocked.)

Becoming Someone Else. Below are two lists. Choose a person from the first list doing an action from the second list. Try to avoid stereotypes. Build your characterization on actual observation rather than on how you think someone does something. Try to imagine what the person is thinking and feeling as he/she acts, too.

your mother or father	eating fried chicken
one of your teachers	putting on a big winter coat
a grandparent	getting into a cold lake or pool
a brother or sister	being confronted by a big dog
your best friend	dropping a hat on a windy day
your worst enemy	putting on shoes and socks
a two-year-old child	getting in a car
a blind person	picking a flower
a very old person	learning a new dance step
someone else you have observed	sneezing
	reading a funny cartoon or hearing a joke
	tripping on a crack or step
	eating a doughnut or roll
	any other action you've observed

On the Job. Observe someone doing his or her work. Watch each step the person goes through in completing a task. In addition, watch for personal reactions and mannerisms the person demonstrates during the task. Then, try to reproduce both the parts of the task and the person's feeling or mood while doing the task (tired? grumpy? cheerful? busy?) Below are some people you might see on the job:

- the gardener at the park
- a barber
- a short-order cook
- a food server at a fast-food restaurant
- a gas-station attendant
- a shoe-store clerk
- a receptionist/secretary
- a bank teller
- a mail carrier
- a pharmacist

Using Your Voice

In the activities above, the focus has been on the use of the body, on facial expression, gesture, posture. An actor also has to project the character he is playing through the use of his voice. Listening to the ways other people talk—their pronunciation, their speed, their rhythm—will give you some ideas about ways you can express a character through the way you talk. The following activities will give you practice in training your voice and in trying out a variety of voices different from your own.

Changing Meanings. People tend to think that the words we say are what make meaning. But how we say what we say has a tremendous influence on our message. "I'm so glad to see you" can be said with a pleasant, friendly voice by someone greeting a friend, with sarcasm by someone irritated by being kept waiting for a long time, or with relief by someone worried about the safety of a friend. Listen to the tone people use when they speak and notice how it affects the meaning of the words.

In addition, practice saying the same sentence in different ways to change its meaning. See how emphasizing a different word each time you say this sentence changes it: "You take that cake."

You take that cake. (Not me or Sarah or Dad.)
You *take* that cake. (Don't buy it; don't leave it here.)
You take *that* cake. (Not *this* one.)
You take that *cake*. (Not the pie or the cookies.)

Here are some more sentences:

I'm getting tired.
Take me home.
Please give me three apples.
I want a motorcycle.
Don't stop at this corner.
Bring in my dog.
My mom bought five kittens.

Try saying one or two simple words in as many ways as you can. See how many messages you can send with the same word.

please	look
thank you	come in
good-bye	OK
sorry	later

Pair up with a friend and take turns guessing what each of you is trying to communicate by the way you say the word.

Matching Sounds. To do this activity you will need a partner. Choose a book or a magazine from which to read aloud. One person reads a sentence aloud from the book and the other one tries to repeat the sentence in exactly the same way—with the same pronunciation, the same emphasis, the same loudness. Take turns mimicking one another. Try out different voices, styles, and accents as you read. A third person might judge whether or not the repeater is saying the sentence exactly as his partner did.

Creating a Character. After you have spent a lot of time listening to the way others talk, try doing some imitations. For example, introduce yourself as if you were

- your math teacher
- a two-year-old child
- your mother
- your best friend
- the gym teacher or coach
- your piano teacher
- a local store clerk
- your worst enemy
- Bugs Bunny or another cartoon character
- Darth Vader or another TV or movie character
- a scientist
- a witch
- your favorite actor or actress

In addition, try giving instructions on how to make a peanut-butter sandwich in the voice of several different characters. Describe your favorite piece of clothing or pastime as other people or characters from TV or movies would.

Projecting Your Voice. Stand facing a partner. Each of you say a sentence and step back a step; continue repeating and moving farther and farther from each other. Try to make yourselves clearly understood without shouting. Try the same activity with whispering.

Imagination

Often, the characters you play when you act are very unlike you, and the situations you are in are different from any experiences you've ever had. In order to understand the character you are playing and to act appropriately as that character, you have to use your imagination. You need to imagine new tastes, new smells, new sights, new sounds, new physical sensations, new emotions. How does it *feel* to be an astronaut in orbit around Mars, to be an old man who is tired and ill, to be a monster created by a mad scientist, to be a woman who has just had a baby, to be the new baby itself? What does it feel like to be alone in a haunted house, robbed by a thief, bucked off a bronco at a rodeo, jilted by your sweetheart?

To imagine, you have to make use of every person and experience you have observed; you need to remember what you have read in books and seen on TV; you need to draw on your *own* experiences. Then you need to make guesses about how people would feel and act and then try to put those guesses into action.

The following is a list of experiences that you have probably never had. Create the actions and reactions of each of the characters in these situations.

• You are an astronaut who has just landed on Mars. Prepare to leave the spaceship; then get out of your ship and explore the area surrounding it.

• You are a sailor on a boat in a storm. Notice the storm coming; make fast attempts to prepare for it; fight it when it hits.

• You are an archeologist trapped in an underground cave. How much light do you have? What can you see? Try to find a way out, at the same time preserving and taking the treasures you have discovered.

• You are a five-year-old child who has just been magically transported to candyland. What all do you see and what will you spend your brief stay doing?

• You are yourself left alone at one of your relative's houses on a deserted street in the country. At midnight, you are awakened by a scratching sound at the back door. What is it and what do you do about it?

As you act out these situations, remember to use your whole body to express both your physical and emotional responses to the situation you are in. Show your reaction with your facial expression, your gestures, your use of your hands, arms, legs, head, shoulders. Begin by trying to imagine the surroundings.

What do you see? Is it dark or light? dreary or beautiful? filled with things to see or bleak? Are you excited, scared, brave, curious about what you see?

What do you hear? Is it silent or noisy? Are there many sounds or just a few repeated over and over? What emotional reaction do you have to the sounds?

Can you smell anything? Is it pleasant? Is it sour? musty? Can you compare it with familiar smells? How do you react to it?

Do you taste anything? React to your tastes.

How do you feel? Hot? cold? tired? heavy? light? tingly? damp? weak? Show your physical reactions with your body.

Pass It Around. Here is a group activity that will help you extend your imaginations. Sit with a group of friends in a large circle. Take turns passing an imaginary object around the circle, giving each person an opportunity to "examine" the object before passing it along to the next person. Every member of the group should get to name an object to pass around the circle. Be sure to use all of your senses in exploring the object. Here are some possibilities:

- a kitten
- a blown-up balloon
- a sharp knife
- a hot potato
- a diamond ring
- an earthworm
- a daisy
- a dirty sock
- a banana peel
- an ice-cream cone
- a lighted candle

What's It For? For this activity, divide into groups of two to four people. Collect several common objects from around the house, and let each group choose one object with which to work. Have each group make a list of all the possible uses their object could serve. How, for example, could you use a Frisbee? It could be a serving dish, a hat, a pot cover, a snow sled for a small animal or elf, a coaster for a large drink, a food dish for a pet, etc. After the groups have finished making their lists, each group makes up a **skit** incorporating as many of the uses on their list as they can. The only prop allowed in the skit is the object the group has chosen. After you have had time to practice the skits, perform them for one another. You might want to let the audience guess what the object is by the way it is used in the skit. Any object will work for this activity, because you use your imaginations to decide what the object becomes, but here are some possibilities:

- a thread spool
- a feather
- a tin can
- a rolling pin
- a corkscrew
- a plastic cup
- a ruler
- a dishrag
- a screwdriver
- a pie pan
- a flowerpot
- a broom

Pantomime

In this section, you will use the skills you have developed in observing and imagining to create **pantomime**—emotions, actions, and events communicated without the use of language. In doing pantomime, an actor must develop concentration, the ability to focus one's thoughts and attention on the use of the body to communicate a message. Everything must be clear through the actor's use of movement, facial expression, and gesture. Every action must be meaningful.

Some Solo Pantomimes. These are pantomimes that are done by one person. If you are with your friends, take turns doing **mimes** and guess what action is being portrayed.

Before you begin your mime, it is important that you have visualized the entire scene and the objects you will be "handling" during the scene. For example, if you are making a peanut-butter sandwich, visualize where everything is kept. Where are the knives? Where are the bread and the peanut butter? Where is the counter or table where you will make the sandwich? Is the peanut better in a tub or jar? How big around is it? Is it hard to unscrew or easy? How many turns do you need? Is the peanut-butter jar nearly full or nearly empty? Do you have to scrape to get enough for your sandwich? What kind of closing, if any, is on the bread bag? Is the bread firm or soft? Do you have any trouble spreading? What do you do with the knife when you are done? the bread? the peanut butter?

The following are simple acts, but they probably take many more movements than you realize, because you do most of them without thinking. Be sure you keep in mind the size, shape, weight, texture, placement in the room of every object you use and encounter.

- eat an apple
- thread a needle and sew a ripped seam
- plant a row of seeds
- set the dinner table
- buy an ice-cream bar from the ice-cream truck
- build a sand castle
- blow up a balloon and tie it
- get dressed for school
- wash and dry your hands and face
- brush your teeth

- feed the dog
- fold a letter, put it in an envelope, seal and stamp it
- fold your clothes and put them in your drawer
- play on a gym set
- change a baby's diapers

Pantomimes for Pairs. These pantomimes are somewhat more complex in that they involve two people interacting with one another. In this case the actors must communicate with one another without the use of words, and it must be clear to the audience what is going on. In these situations, there will also be more of a need to express emotion with your mime. You may want to do a little advanced preparation before you begin your mime, or you might want to improvise.

- shoe salesman trying shoes on a customer
- mother or father feeding baby something he doesn't want
- store clerk and customer arguing because customer thinks he has been shortchanged
- child wants Mom to buy candy
- Mom wants child to mow the lawn
- one person in a lake trying to get his friend to come in
- child breaks glass and is scolded by mother
- two kids arguing about what television show to watch
- young girl and boy leaving to go out on their first date
- two people arguing about who caused an automobile accident

The message of these mimes are not as easily shown as the specific actions in the solo mime. Think about action, gesture, and facial expressions that will make your meaning clear to your audience. Take turns performing and guess what is being acted out.

Place Pantomimes. This is a good activity to do in small groups with three to five members. After you have divided into groups, spend a few minutes deciding on a setting. The other groups guess what place you are in by your actions. Do a little advance planning to decide what role each of you will have in this place, but let the pantomime develop spontaneously.

Some possible places:

- an elegant restaurant
- a fast-food place
- your own dining room
- a canoe
- a sailboat
- an ocean liner
- an amusement park
- a zoo
- a museum
- a cave
- a haunted house
- a movie theater
- a baseball game
- a grocery store
- a clothes store
- a candy store
- an airplane
- a train
- an open field
- a forest
- a doctor's office
- a dentist's office
- a barber shop

Pantomime Stories. Using settings from the above list, develop pantomimes into longer scenes, selecting an event that occurs at that particular place. Beginning with the setting, decide on a conflict or problem that arises there and is somehow resolved. For example:

- Mom and Dad realize that one of their four children is no longer with them at the zoo or amusement park.
- A restaurant patron refuses to pay the check because the food was cold.
- The child won't let the doctor check his nose or ears during his medical exam.
- Two children get lost in a forest.
- A woman is terrified of planes and won't let go of the stranger sitting next to her.

Think up other situations that can occur in the settings.

Fairy Tale Pantomimes. Act out scenes from your favorite fairy tale, nursery rhyme, or children's story for the children in your neighborhood. Use:

Goldilocks and the Three Bears
Cinderella
Hansel and Gretel
Sleeping Beauty
Three Billy Goats Gruff
Little Red Riding Hood
The Princess and the Pea
Rumpelstiltskin
Mary Had a Little Lamb
Jack and Jill
Little Bo-Peep
Jack Sprat
Jack Be Nimble
Old Mother Hubbard
The Old Woman Who Lived in a Shoe
Tom, Tom, the Piper's Son

Baa, Baa, Black Sheep
Little Boy Blue
Hey Diddle, Diddle
Peter, Peter, Pumpkin Eater

Poetry Pantomimes. Some poems tell stories. Other poems express feelings, create pictures, or communicate a mood. Choose a poem that you would like to act out in pantomime. Depending on the poem, you may want to do individual pantomimes or group pantomimes. Choose one person to read the poem. Create actions that communicate the message or express the mood of the poem. Practice miming as someone else reads so that you are able to coordinate the words and the actions before you perform your pantomime for an audience.

There are many collections of poetry available in the library. Here are some that you might like to look for:

Storytelling Poems
Story Poems Old and New edited by William Cole
100 More Story Poems edited by Elinor Parker
John Brown's Body by Stephen Vincent Benet (a long ballad about the
    American Civil War)

Humorous Poems
The Fireside Book of Humorous Poetry edited by William Cole
The Moon Is Shining Bright as Day edited by Ogden Nash
Where the Sidewalk Ends by Shel Silverstein

General Collections
An Inheritance of Poetry edited by Gladys Adshead and Annis Duff
Reflections on a Gift of Watermelon Pickle and *Some Haystacks
    Don't Even Have Any Needle* edited by Stephen Dunning, Edward
    Lueders, and Hugh Smith
The Family Book of Verse edited by Lewis S. Gannett
Wonders and Surprises edited by Phyllis McGinley

Pantomimes to Music. Earlier in this chapter we recommended music for free movement and warm-up. Music can also suggest a story. Choose a piece of music which has several changes in rhythm and mood. Listen to it carefully and jot down ideas for actions that seem to fit the feeling of the music. Plot a story which uses the actions that you have come up with. Practice the story and perform it for an audience.

chapter 2

Plays Without Scripts

Many theatrical presentations are based on a **script**, a written-out version of the play with specific lines for the actors and actresses to memorize. Before you have finished using this book, we hope that you will write a complete scripted play. But writing a script (and then having the actors and actresses memorize the lines) can require a great deal of time and energy. Further, it is not always necessary to have a script to put on a good play. In this chapter we will show you plays *without* scripts, simply using your imagination to create a play with little or no advance planning.

Games That Are Plays

In her book, *Children's Games from Many Lands* (New York: Friendship Press, 1965), Nina Millen shows that young people all over the world play games that are very much like skits or plays. In the Congo, for example, children play a game called "Antelope in the Net," where a person becomes "it" and plays the antelope, while the rest of the players make a "net" of their hands and try to keep the antelope from escaping. Does that game sound vaguely familiar? We've seen young people in the United States playing the same game, only they called it "Horse in the Corral," with one person pretending to be a captured wild horse as the rest of the group tries to keep him or her inside a corral or fence of arms.

In Turkey, children play "Fox and Hen." One player—the hen—holds her arms outstretched to protect other players—her brood—from a fox who tries to sneak around and grab off a chick for his dinner. In America, kids play a game with the same name but with a different "drama": The "chickens" line up on one side of a room or playground and, at a signal, rush to the other side, trying to avoid being snatched by the fox.

Sometimes games are "plays" that are actual imitations of life. For instance, a simple game like "Hide and Go Seek" involves acting out one of humankind's oldest occupations: hunting. The Cheyenne Indians play a variation of hide and seek that imitates a bear hunt. In that game, the person who is "it" pretends to be the bear and hides, while everybody else plays hunters who try to find the bear. If it sees a hunter, the bear may leap out of hiding and pretend to attack, and the rest of the hunters rush to the aid of their comrade, just as they would in real life. Thus you can see how this game—this "play"—reflects a traditional part of Cheyenne life.

Games can also involve acting out myths and legends. In China, children play a game based on the importance of the dragon in their folklore. The players form a line, each person placing hands on another person's shoulders, to make a long dragon. The head then chases the tail, trying to catch the tail without causing the dragon to break apart. The Chippewa Indians play a variation of the bear-hunt game called "The Windigo," named after an ancient and frightening spirit that is said to haunt the woods of North America. The person who is "it" (the Windigo) hides while others try to find him or her. If the Windigo can sneak up on a person without being seen, that person is transformed into a spirit and must join with the Windigo. If the hunters spot the Windigo first, its power is destroyed.

Even the familiar game of "Tag" has its origins in myth and legend. The touch of a spirit was said to be evil, contaminating a person and making him or her "it." When we were younger, kids on our block played a variation called "Poison Tag," where the touch of the person who was it "poisoned" you, and you had to hold onto your arm or knee or wherever you had been touched.

Many games are "plays" about an adult activity that is not a game at all—*war*. We used to play a game called "War": One kid would bounce a tennis ball on the street or playground, sending it as high in the air as he could, while calling out "I make war on _____(name)_____." The person whose name was called would catch the ball and shout, "Stop!", causing the other players to freeze. Then that person would throw the ball, trying to hit the nearest person. If the thrower were successful, he or she took a footprint-sized patch of land from the other person's "territory," sketched in chalk on the street. If the thrower missed, then the other person won a chunk of land, just as in a real war countries struggle over territory.

Even some sports are games that are a little like plays. Football, for example, is a war play, where the characters—the *play*-ers—struggle over land, pushing each other backward and forward. Incidentally, football originated as a sort of war game played between whole towns, with the townspeople trying to force the citizens of one town back inside their own town limits.

Now, for some readers of this book, the games we have been describing are part of your past history. You don't play "Tag" or "Hide and Go Seek" anymore—that's something for younger kids. But you probably play other kinds of games, and if you think about it, you'll see they are also like plays. For example, you have probably played "Monopoly," a game in which people pretend to be financiers in search of wealth. Who can forget the dramatic excitement when some player lands on the "Go Directly to Jail" square and heads off to the slammer instead of around "Go"? Another unusually popular game with older young folks is "Dungeons and Dragons," which involves make-believe and fantasy with wizards, dragons, buried treasure, intrigue, and treachery.

Remember, too, that all these plays are plays without scripts. The players simply pick out the parts they will play or choose up sides, and the game (or play) begins.

Whether you're young or older, you enjoy playing games of one kind or another. One way to begin the activities in this chapter is simply to make a list of your favorite games and then *play them*. As you do, think about how the game is like a drama. Who are the main characters? What is the plot?

You might also enjoy inventing some play/games yourself. Here are some ideas for games that will get you started.

Wizard's Den. This is a variation of a game we played as kids; it was called "Statues." For this game, the Wizard sits on a chair, beneath which the treasure has been placed (a rock will do nicely). The other players line up in the distance and try to sneak up on the Wizard, who turns suddenly and unexpectedly. The players "freeze," for if the Wizard sees any person move, that person is put under a spell and disqualified. Eventually someone makes it all the way to the Wizard's den and swipes the treasure.

The Alien Touch. This is a variation of the Indian "Bear Hunt" and "Windigo" games. One person is the Alien, a grotesque outer-space creature (you can make up the description of what it's like). The touch of the Alien turns people into its own kind. If the Alien can sneak up on a space explorer and touch him or her, that person must join the Alien forces and join in the hunt for other spacepeople. As the game progresses, the Aliens grow more and more in number and threaten to take over the universe. However, if a spaceperson can sneak up on an Alien, the Alien is "destroyed" and must leave the game. Who will rule the universe?

The Quest. The story of King Arthur and his Knights of the Round Table is well known. This game represents the Knights' search for the Holy Grail, the cup from which Jesus is said to have drunk. Merlin, the evil magician, steals the Grail (which can be represented by a rock or by an actual cup) and hides it. Under King Arthur's direction, the Knights search for the Grail, but their search is complicated by Merlin, who gives out some false and some true hints about where the Grail can be found.

Space Shuttle. One person is "it" and stands in the middle playing the role of the Enemy Satellite. The other players are space vehicles—Shuttles—that must go from planet to planet delivering goods. Each "planet" is a safe place, represented by a tree (if you're outdoors), a chair (if you're inside), or a small sheet of cardboard placed on the ground or the floor. The trick to this game is that there is one more space shuttle than there are planets, so one Shuttle must always be on the move, going to a new planet. The Enemy Satellite tries to catch the Shuttles as they run from planet to planet. Sound familiar? This is a variation of two old favorite games: "Fox and Hens" and "Musical Chairs."

Charades. This is a very popular party game in which one person or a group of people act out an idea or scene while others try to guess the idea. For example, try a game of Charades based on comic strips. If you were trying to represent "Peanuts," you might have one person roleplay Snoopy, another be Woodstock, a third and fourth represent Lucy and Charlie Brown. You could play Charades based on superheroes. How would you act out Spiderman? the Hulk? Batman and Robin? Wonder Woman? Superman? Charades can also be done about holidays. How would you act out Thanksgiving Day? Valentine's Day? Independence Day (the 4th of July)? Finally, Charades can also be played on famous sayings. How would you present such maxims as:

"A rolling stone gathers no moss."
"Too many cooks spoil the broth."
"Children should be seen and not heard."
"Haste makes waste."

Board Games. Here is a rainy-day activity to help relieve boredom. Invent a new game that can be played indoors, using a "board" like Monopoly or Checkers. To make a game all you need is a sheet of cardboard or posterboard, a few sheets of paper, some buttons or spools to represent players, and perhaps some dice or a spinner to determine moves. Almost any of the games we have described so far can be played on a board. For example, "The Windigo" could be done with several trails leading through a forest, with plenty of traps to catch people. The Windigo can be represented by certain squares on the board. If you land on one, you must go to the Windigo's lair, lose a turn, and go back to the beginning. How people move is determined by a roll of the dice. The first player to make it through the forest is the winner.

Other Games. Here are some titles for other games that are plays. You make up the rules—the "play." These can be done on a game board or for real in the out-of-doors. Once you have developed a set of rules, round up some kids and play the game.

Auto Race	Cat and Mouse
The Jungle	Streets and Alleys
Gangsters	Nice Guys
Track Meet	Stamp Collectors
Robin Hood	Hospital
Survival	Pizza Party

Drama with Puppets

Puppetry is one of the oldest forms of drama. In his *Complete Book of Puppetry* (Boston: Plays, Inc., 1974), David Currell shows that puppets may have been used in India over four thousand years ago, and it is certain the Chinese used puppets over two thousand years ago. Puppets were a source of drama in ancient Greece and Rome; the idea was passed along through the countries of Europe and eventually reached us by way of Great Britain.

Your own introduction to puppetry may well have been through television where three shows, in particular, make use of puppets to entertain youngsters: *Sesame Street, Captain Kangaroo,* and *Mister Rogers.* But you probably saw "live" puppet shows when you were a child: at school, at the library, maybe even on a street corner or at a carnival. And certainly you have played with puppets, perhaps some puppets you have been given as gifts.

We enjoy puppetry as a form of neighborhood theater because almost every person we know enjoys playing with puppets, and people often discover new directions in their dramatic talent when they put on a puppet and make a play. Somehow having that object on your hand to talk "through" makes it easier for you to relax and be dramatic. We've seen people who were very shy about appearing on stage figuratively explode when they engaged in puppetry, losing all their inhibitions. Further, having a puppet on your hand provides you with a point of focus that makes concentration much easier.

Not the least of the fun is the actual making of puppets. Even if you don't think you have a lot of artistic talent, you can succeed at making an entire **repertory company** of strange and wonderful creatures. And making puppets need not be very expensive.

Entire books have been written about puppet making, so we won't go into that in much detail, simply suggesting a few basic and cheap kinds of puppets to get you started.

The Human Hand. Make a quacking motion with your left hand while you talk in a low voice. Make a quacking motion with your right hand and talk in a high voice. Let High Voice and Low Voice have a conversation, and you're on your way—puppetry with your bare hand. If you want to get more elaborate, you can take lipstick and/or a grease pencil, make a few markings for eyes and lips, and you have another hand puppet as shown in Figure 1.

Finger Puppets. These "mini-puppets" are fun because they are quick to make and easy to use. A finger puppet slips over your finger (or thumb), and if you get good enough, you can operate ten finger puppets at once, giving you a great crowd. To make one, simply roll a square of paper, light cardboard, or felt into a tube (Figure 2) and add facial expressions. Finger

FIGURE 1

THE HUMAN HAND: UNADORNED

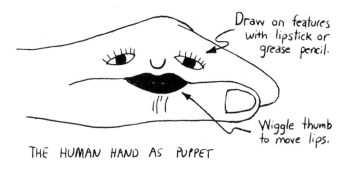

Draw on features with lipstick or grease pencil.

Wiggle thumb to move lips.

THE HUMAN HAND AS PUPPET

puppets also make a nice gift to present to younger children, and you can teach them how to put on puppet plays.

Paper Bag Puppets. Also inexpensive and easy are puppets made from plain paper bags, usually bags the size of lunch sacks (Figure 3). Paper bags can be made into all sorts of people or animals, and you can make them quite elaborate by adding decorations of pasted-on paper, cloth, buttons, glitter, and so on.

For more complex kinds of puppets and marionettes, head for the library and check out a good book on puppet making.

Puppet Plays. Once you've made yourself some puppets, let the play—the drama—begin. You don't need to structure a puppet play too carefully. Often the characters will do that for you, and as soon as you have the pup-

FINGER PUPPETS

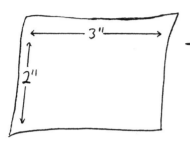

← 1. START WITH A RECTANGLE OF PAPER OR CLOTH.

3"

2"

2. ROLL IT INTO A TUBE AND GLUE SEAM.

Glue here

3. ADD FEATURES. GLUE ON PAPER OR FELT SCRAPS, OR DRAW WITH FELT-TIP PEN.

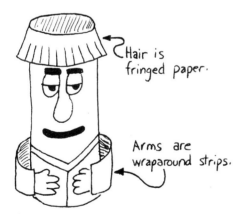

Hair is fringed paper.

Arms are wraparound strips.

OTHER IDEAS:

Fold over tube

Yarn

FIGURE 2

BAGERODS

1. RECYCLE YOUR LUNCH BAGS. A PAPER BAG IS BUILT SOMETHING LIKE THIS.

Yarn or ribbon for hair.

2. IF YOU PUT EYES ON TOP (ACTUALLY THE BOTTOM OF THE BAG), THE FOLD BECOMES A TALKING MOUTH.

Clothing and face are drawn on or cut from paper and pasted on.

3. TUCK THE EYES UNDERNEATH. PUT THE EYELIDS ON TOP AND YOU GET A PUPPET THAT WILL BLINK.

FIGURE 3

pet on your hand, the play will begin. You may want to have some sort of stage so the puppeteers are hidden from the audience. Pulling a couch out from the wall and hiding behind it works well. So does tipping a table on its side (with permission) and working from behind it. If you want to build a somewhat more complex puppet stage, see the instructions given in Part II of this book.

Free Play. Let the characters spontaneously grow into a drama. Just put on the puppets and let them have a conversation with each other. You can do this yourself, with one puppet on your right hand and one on your left, or you can do it with a friend, using up to four puppets.

Storytelling. Have someone read one of your favorite stories (or the favorite of a younger brother or sister) aloud. While the person reads, act out the story with your puppets. As a variation, have the person stop reading in the middle of the story, and you create a new and different ending. Or invite your audience to suggest some new and interesting endings. (What if the Little Red Hen's friends had actually helped her bake that bread?)

Television Shows. Make puppets to represent the characters of your favorite television shows: cartoons, children's shows, comedies, soap operas, adventures, and so forth. Then put on your own versions of the show.

Puppet Dance. Since most puppets don't have any feet, you may be surprised to realize that you can have them dance. Select a piece of music you like, preferably a song or part of a symphony without words. Play the record, then have your puppets sway and dance with the music, capturing its mood for your audience.

Historical Plays. Create puppets to reenact important events in history: the Boston Tea Party, the first Thanksgiving, the signing of the Declaration of Independence. (This is a project you may want to develop for school.)

Tidings of_____?_____. Have one person (puppet) be a bringer of news. Good news. Bad news. Good news *and* bad news. How do the other characters respond? What do they say? Let the play grow from there.

Other starting points for puppet plays include:

- A photographer trying to get a family to sit still for a portrait.
- The reunion of a family whose members haven't seen each other for years. (As a variation, make puppets to represent the members of your own family and hold a reunion.)
- A telephone operator trying to handle calls from three or four people at once and connecting people with the wrong parties. (If you have several puppeteers for this one, place them in several corners of the room as if they were calling from different parts of town or different parts of the country.)
- A pack of dogs, locked in the pound, planning their escape.
- A gathering of dragons discussing what havoc they will wreak on the humans.
- An assembly of Martians considering some tricks to play on the earthlings.

Making Up a Play as You Go Along

We hope that the previous sections on games and puppetry have convinced you that you are already good at making up a play as you go along. But in case you need more persuading, you should also remember that just playing "make believe" is also a form of drama, whether playing with dolls or playing "let's pretend" about school or home. There is also a form of theater which is based on make-believe, so "pretending" is not something that is childish or for the very young. This form of theater is called **improvisation,** and there are whole theater companies that specialize in it. (The best known is the Second City company in Chicago.) People in the audience are invited to suggest ideas for skits, and the actors and actresses come up with a skit on the spur of the moment.

The members of a troupe like Second City are experienced professionals who have been working with one another for years. But you and your friends can, with a little practice, become excellent at improvisation, too. You'll need to know that a skit must contain at least three parts or elements:

First, the **setting.** This is simply the place where the drama will happen.

It can be a real place or an imaginary place. Some good settings for improvised plays are:

Crowded department store	School classroom
Jail	A bus
Your home	Police station
Prehistoric times	A city street
A dungeon	The enchanted forest
A castle	A desert island
A dark alley	A country road
Haunted house	On a tree limb

Next you need some **characters.** These are the basic people (or animals or monsters or other living things) that make up your drama. It's important that your characters have *character,* which means that they must have strong personalities. Often your setting will suggest the characters. If you're going to do a play about a castle, then *knights,* a *king* and *queen,* and perhaps some *servants* will be the main characters. If your setting is the police station, you'll need police officers and people suspected of a crime. Sometimes you can work backward, and your characters will suggest a setting for the play. Here are some characters that may get you started.

Baby	Spy	Student
Old person	Artist	Butcher
Martian	Master criminal	Baker
Parent	Superhero(ine)	Coach
Grandparent	Animal	Engineer
Police chief	Dragon	Elf
Sports hero	Prince(ss)	Ship captain
Movie star	Fairy	Airline pilot
Rock singer	Goblin	Dinosaur

Last, you will need some sort of **conflict** or problem to make your play move along. For example, a sports hero might be in conflict with his or her coach about how to play the big game. Two dinosaurs are in conflict about whether to move south for the winter. A movie star and a rock star disagree over whether records or films are more interesting or more important. Your play does *not* have to be all argument. It could involve a problem like a sinking ship, a time bomb, or a witch who is fouling up television reception. The important thing is that the conflict or problem forces your characters to deal with each other. Some conflicts:

Some property is missing. Who took it?
Two people are in love with the same girl or boy.
I saw it first!
Time stands still.
The car breaks down in the middle of nowhere.
The dam has broken.

To create an improvised drama, follow these basic steps:

1) *Choose your setting and your characters.* You can use our ideas or come up with some of your own. Sometimes the character combinations can be wacky (a superheroine, a Martian, and an elf) and your setting can be very strange or exotic (inside the petals of a giant flower).

2) *Think of a conflict or problem.* "The dam has broken!" "But I love you, too."

3) *Plan your play.* You don't have to do a lot of planning, but huddle with your actors and actresses for a minute to make plans. If your stage is the living room, imagine how the furniture fits your setting. ("Let's have the couch be a bus seat and drag over the easy chair for the bus driver's seat.") Spend a minute talking with one another about what you think *might* happen. (Remember, you don't have to plan everything in advance. Part of the fun is in making up the play as you go along.) Think about a **climax,** a time when the argument or conflict is at its peak, and then think about a way to bring that conflict to a **resolution** or ending. (The villagers learn of the flood just in time and escape. The two quarreling lovers patch up their differences.)

Just before you begin, spend thirty seconds in silence, with the actors and actresses thinking about their roles. How will *you*—the captain, the parent, the bratty kid—react to what happens? Get everyone in the mood to play their roles.

Then make a play! Be your characters. Enjoy the drama for as long as you want, then let it come to an end.

Improvisations for One Person

You've probably heard about a "one-man show" or "one-woman show" on Broadway. That can be among the most challenging kinds of theater for an actress or actor to do, standing in front of an audience for up to two hours and being the center of attention. You won't want to be on stage that long (at first, in any case), but you might like to use improvisation as a way of putting on a one-person show of your own. You can develop a single improvisation, or perhaps choose several from the list of suggestions in this section.

A one-person show can be a silent play—a **pantomime**—as we discussed in the previous chapter. However, we suggest that you try something called a **dramatic monologue,** which is a fancy way of saying, "talking to yourself." The dramatic monologue is a very old and well-accepted convention of the theater, and it simply means that the actor or actress puts his or her thoughts into words so the audience can hear them. You'll catch on quickly as you try these ideas for one-person improvisations.

Telephone Conversation. This improvisation is an easy way to get started. Pretend you are holding a telephone—or get a phone and use it as a **prop**—and imagine that you are holding a conversation with another person. You might be:

- a student away at college talking with his/her parents.
- having a lovers' quarrel with your girlfriend or boyfriend.

- arguing with a person to whom you owe money, or who owes you money.
- talking with your doctor about your health.

As you roleplay, remember to pause while you listen to the other person talk. Imagine what he or she is saying and let your facial expressions and your body show your reaction. Then respond—aloud—just as you would over the telephone. Remember to build the drama to a climax, then bring it to a close. Your hanging up the phone signals the fall of the final curtain.

The Mysterious Package. This improvisation begins with you going to the door to receive a package from a delivery person. "What could it be?" you wonder aloud to yourself. Pantomime unwrapping the package, all the while talking to yourself about what you think might be inside and who sent it to you. Bring the play to a close by revealing to the audience what's in the box. (No bombs, please!)

Historical Character. Many of the Broadway one-person shows have involved an actor or actress turning into an historical character for a night, for example, the author Mark Twain or President Harry S. Truman. Begin by selecting a character from history you admire or who interests you; then go to the library and check out a biography or autobiography about that person. Read up on your character's life; then, on stage, become that person and tell some of his or her stories to your audience. Or, let people interview you, asking you questions about "your" life. If you'd like, find out the kinds of clothing the person wore and dress up to fit the part.

Time Machine. This one also may involve some library reading. Pick an era that interests you, a time from the recent or distant past: the Civil War years, the Roman era, even prehistoric times. Get a book about that time and read up on it. Then, for your improvisation, explain to your audience that you have been transported back in time and will tell them about what you see.

Gulliver. In Jonathan Swift's book, *Gulliver's Travels*, an Englishman, Gulliver, is shipwrecked on the island of Lilliput, inhabited by people only a few inches tall. While he sleeps on the beach, the Lilliputians tie him to the ground, and he wakes up to find little people swarming all over him. Be Gulliver on stage and have a dramatic monologue with the Lilliputians.

High Diver. In pantomime you climb the many steps up a swaying ladder to the diver's platform, high above the crowd. You look down at the pool into which you are to dive, and it looks like a tiny blue puddle. Suddenly you freeze. No way are you going to jump off that platform! The crowd grows restless and starts shouting things at you. You shout back. An argument takes place. Does the diver take the plunge or not? You decide. (In another variation of this roleplay, become a *tightrope walker* who becomes frightened halfway across.)

Auto Mechanic. You pretend to roll under your customer's car, lying on your back on a mechanic's "creeper" cart. From underneath the automobile, you shout to the customer about what's wrong with the car. Use lots of mumbo-jumbo and technical talk to describe what's wrong.

Steam-Roller Operator. Ever wonder what it would be like to operate one of those huge rollers that flatten out earth and asphalt? Now's the time to find out. Imagine yourself seated high in the driver's seat while the construction project proceeds beneath you. Roll forward and back, back and forward, all the time calling out instructions and orders to the worker below. Look out! Don't run over that fireplug by accident. . . .

Other Ideas. Just about any character (or even object) that you imagine can have a dramatic monologue in front of an audience. For a moment of theater, become:

- King Arthur's sword, Excalibur
- an ambulance driver
- a lost dog or lost child
- a detective puzzling over a clue
- your favorite TV star
- your favorite TV character
- a goldfish in a tank

Scenes for Two People

Working with one other actor or actress presents some interesting possibilities for drama. When working with only one person, you can develop a strong relationship or partnership so you can learn to "play off" your partner in ways that aren't possible in larger groups. Also, it's easier to get a two-person drama started because you don't have to round up a huge acting crew. Remember as you start the improvisation to spend time concentrating, thinking about what you want the characters to be, where you want the drama to take place, how you want it to end. Try some of the following ideas for two-person plays.

The Salesperson and the Customer. This play is a classic in theater and in the movies. One person roleplays the salesperson, who is trying to sell his or her wares. The other person is the reluctant customer who has to be persuaded. Some variations of this skit include:

- the used-car salesman trying to persuade the customer that an old clunker is really a pretty good deal.
- the vacuum-cleaner salesman who dumps a bag of dirt on somebody's living room rug and offers to clean it up.
- trying to sell sombody something he or she doesn't need, like a machine that will peel 2000 potatoes an hour or a subscription to a magazine for bricklayers.

The Complicated Conversation. The comedians Lou Abbott and Bud Costello used to do a routine about a baseball player named "Who." "Who's on first," one comedian would say as a statement. "That's what I want to know, too," said his partner, getting confused. As the conversation grew more and more complicated, it became funnier and funnier. Some variations on this complicated conversation include:

- A request for help that gets very complex:
  HE: Will you get me my sweater?
  SHE: Sure, which one?

HE: The blue one.

SHE: The blue one with white designs?

HE: No, the blue one with the yellow alligator.

SHE: Oh, sure, where is it?

HE: In the drawer.

SHE: Which drawer?

and so on.

- Directions that get complicated:

  JACK: I'll be right over. How do I get to your house?

  JILL: It's easy. Come down Main Street and take your third left. No, maybe it's the fourth. In any case, it's Mulberry Street. Or you could turn left on Vine if you wanted to. Then come down about a quarter mile to the intersection where the drug store was before they tore it down. . . .

- An "I can top that" tall tale or argument:

  WILLY: My boss just told me I do good work.

  NILLY: Terrific, but my boss just told me that he couldn't get along without me.

  WILLY: That's great, but *my* boss said he wants me to help him make all the crucial decisions.

  NILLY: That's interesting, but my boss even wants me to go on vacation with him so I can help him out then.

  and so on.

Problems and Deep Troubles. Two people get into a difficult situation and have to figure a way out:

- two window washers are trapped on a ledge on the fiftieth floor of the building after everybody has gone home. How do they get back inside?

- two mountain climbers get themselves up, but can't get down.

Playmaking   **41**

- two deep-sea divers either A) run out of air or B) are captured by a giant clam.
- a pair of identical twins forgets which one is which.

Confrontations. Earlier we said that conflict is one of the keys to success in drama. You must have some conflict in order for the play to take place. Try some of the following scenes of conflict for two people:

- A person returns something to a store, having actually used it. The salesperson refuses to accept soiled merchandise. A confrontation ensues.
- A teacher goes to the principal to complain about the bad behavior of a class. The principal replies, "Don't be silly. Just get back in there and teach!"
- A hair stylist or barber does a terrible job on a customer's head.
- A taxi driver and a customer get into an argument about the best way to get from here to there.
- A couple, packing for a trip, accuse each other of bringing along so many clothes that their suitcases are overfilled.
- A talking dog decides it is no longer interested in being its master's best friend.
- A customer at an ice-cream store says to the clerk, "No, no. You got it wrong. I wanted the scoop of pistachio fudge ripple on *top* of the strawberry bubblegum, not underneath it."
- An optometrist (eye doctor) gets into an argument with a customer over whether he/she needs glasses.

What Ifs. Roleplay what might happen if:

- George Washington met Abraham Lincoln.
- Batman and Robin got fed up with the whole thing.
- Two house painters discover they've each painted one wall a different color.

Putting on a Play

- A girlfriend and boyfriend realize it's all over between them, but neither wants to be the one to say, "Let's break up."

Three or More's a Crowd

As we move into improvised dramas that involve three or more people, things start to get more complicated. In a one- or two-person show, it's easy to get agreement as to what is going to happen. When a number of people are involved, that's not so easy. If your play is to be a good one, then, you will have to take special care to organize and plan.

For plays involving three or more, you may want to consider having somebody (probably *you*) serve as the **director**—the boss who makes decisions and helps people organize. You don't want to seem bossy, of course, and being director does not keep you from participating in the play.

The director should help assign the parts. How many characters will there be in your plan? How many actors and actresses do you have? Try to match people to parts so that all your cast is happy. (Sometimes you will have to invent parts so everybody can participate in the play. Other times, you may have to have an actor or actress take on more than one role.)

Then discuss what will happen in the play. How will it begin? Who's on stage first? When do other characters enter? What will people say? Again, in improvised drama you don't have to know *exactly* what everyone will say word for word, but you should have a pretty good idea how the speeches will go. You might want to lead your cast in a **walk through** or a full-scale **rehearsal** before you actually perform the play for an audience.

Here are some ideas for plays involving three or more actors and actresses:

Nursery Stories. For a younger audience, familiar tales are also enjoyable as plays, and they're good for beginning actors and actresses because everybody knows how the story ends. Ask the members of your cast to think of their favorite nursery stories. Then pick one and work out plans for the play. Good stories for dramatization include: *The Three Little Pigs,*

Goldilocks and the Three Bears, Hansel and Gretel, Little Red Riding Hood, and *The Little Red Hen.*

Melodrama. Melodrama is a kind of adventure theater with all the parts exaggerated. The villain (there is *always* a villain) is evil and rotten to the core, a person so mean that dogs are afraid to bite him (or, sometimes, her). The hero is such a good person he is squeaky clean, a tough-but-gentle person who fights fair and always has good table manners. The heroine is a sweet young thing, stereotypically feminine, all smiles and perfume and lace. In melodrama these characters and others fight and feud until the hero overcomes the villain (at least for now).

Some ideas and characters for melodrama:

A Bank Robbery. The villain and his gang rob a bank and seize a sweet young bank teller as hostage. The hero (the teller's fiancé?) manages to rescue the girl, save the bank, and is rewarded for his troubles.

The Forced Marriage. A wiley and crafty villain promises to give his daughter in marriage to another wiley and despicable villain. The hero interrupts their plans and wins the maiden's hand and heart.

You Must Pay the Rent. The villain is a vicious landlord about to throw the heroine, a widow, out on the street along with her three children just because she can't come up with the rent on time. Enter the hero to save the day.

Will the Train Be on Time? In this classic melodrama, the villain ties the heroine to the railroad tracks. (Who knows why? He just likes to do that sort of thing.) Arriving in the nick of time, the hero rescues the girl and saves the day. (If you'd like, have him save the train as well, stopping it before it plunges into a gorge.)

Reverse Melodrama. Having tried a regular melodrama, reverse some of the roles. Make the hero a girl—a smart, attractive, sensible person who gets her boyfriend—a real loser—out of all sorts of scrapes. Let the villain be a woman instead of a man.

Other ideas for improvisations include:

The Robot Family. A day in the life of the Robots, a family that looks like a collection of over-sized soup cans.

The Flying Carpet. Set your play on the fibers of an imaginary flying carpet that takes you and your cast all over the world as a team of international troubleshooters, solving problems wherever they arise.

Mutiny on the Bounty. A sailing ship is in trouble, tossed about the seas by a violent typhoon and being run by a captain who seems to have lost his marbles. The crew members get together and decide what to do. Should they mutiny and risk life in prison to save the ship? Can they talk the crazy captain back to sanity?

The Lion Tamer. A lion tamer runs up against some rebellious lions who are sick of standing on their hind legs and jumping through fiery hoops. They decide to run the show.

Don't Open That Door, Please. A real-estate salesperson is trying to sell a house with a skeleton in the closet—a real skeleton.

Decisions, Decisions. It's time for the Princess to get married. To decide among her various suitors, she puts them to an odd series of tests, such as finding a french-fried bagel, a plant that grows upside down, or a 1953 Spiderman comic book.

Problem/Solution Plays. In this improvisation, the characters actually try to solve a problem that the play director poses for them. The characters pretend that the problem is a real one and discuss how they would go about finding a solution. For example, problem/solution plays might include:

The Broken Window. Having accidentally smashed the window of a grouchy neighbor, a group of kids decide what to do.

The Pollution Solution. The Board of Directors of United General Corporation is told that its smokestacks are polluting the environment. Fixing the stacks would be very expensive, and the company is on shaky financial grounds. What should the directors do?

The Elevator Dilemma. An elevator gets stuck between floors. The passengers may include: a woman who is about to have a baby, a man who needs to take a pill (and the pills are in his office), someone who is claustrophobic (afraid of being enclosed in small places), and a man with a basketful of snakes. What do they do?

Problem/solution plays can also be done for real. For example, what are some of the problems that are facing the town or city where you live? Roleplay the town council and make suggestions for solutions. If a group of kids is having an argument, have them roleplay themselves and work out real solutions to their problems. In this way, your playmaking can become quite realistic and helpful.

Plays That Involve Everybody (Including the Audience)

Now get everybody into the act! In this section we'll supply ideas for plays that have no "audience," where everybody in the room or theater has a part to play. These are interesting plays to use at the beginning of a party as guests arrive, with a room decorated as the set for the play. As people come in, they figure out what is happening in the play and join in, thus getting acquainted with other people who are present.

To organize an "everybody play," first sit down and make a list of all the characters who might be present in your drama. For example, if you were going to do a play set in a shopping mall, you could list all the people who might be around: shoppers, kids, security guards, shopkeepers, custodians, and so on.

Then think about some sort of interesting plot or incident, something that would draw all the people together and focus their attention. For example, at a shopping mall, there might be a robbery or a lost child that would cause people to talk and interact with one another.

Finally, come up with a way to end the play or resolve the conflict: the robber is caught (or gets away), the little child finds its mother or father. After that, people go about their business as usual.

Some ideas for whole group plays:

The Restaurant. Your lead actor will be the headwaiter, who assigns people to tables, where they pretend to go through the ritual of dining: reading the menu, eating dinner, ordering dessert, and so on. You'll need some waiters and waitresses, and, of course, some customers. For this drama to work, encourage your actors and actresses to start a modest amount of trouble. "Waiter, there's a fly in my soup!" "Sir, will you please stop smoking that cigar?!" "My steak is too tough!" "Oh, I've spilled wine on my blouse!"

Airplane 198? Seat actors and actresses two by two in a long row to represent an airplane. Place a pilot and copilot at the head of the row. Then let trouble develop: *The plane is running out of fuel. A hijacker says there's a bomb aboard. A woman starts having her baby. A stewardess gets sick and tired of being nice to people.* As confusion mounts, the copilot tries to keep people calm and happy.

Lazy Days at the Fishing Hole. Your actors and actresses line up in a long row, sitting side by side, pretending to be fishing. This "play" can simply consist of conversation of an ordinary sort, interrupted from time to time as somebody catches something or gets a bite. Or you can turn it into an adventure: "Is that the fin of a giant shark I see breaking out of the waters of Peaceful Pond?"

Zoo. In this improvisation, half your players pretend to be animals; half become visitors to the zoo. Include a collection of funny animals—like the monkeys and the tortoises—and some oddball visitors: overeager photographers, a nasty little kid who pesters the animals, a person who is terrified the lions will get loose.

Sporting Event. Let your imagination loose in creating the cast for a football, basketball, baseball, or other game. You'll need coaches, players, fans, and maybe a marching band, cheerleaders, and a flag corps.

Pearly Whites. Arrange people in a half circle and have them roleplay a set of teeth. Other characters in this play can be a toothbrush, a stalk of celery, and mean old Mr. Tooth Decay.

Mother Nature Strikes Back. One actor roleplays a gardener in his or her greenhouse. The rest of the group becomes plants that have suddenly turned hostile and are attacking the gardener. Or do the same idea set in the imaginary out-of-doors, with half your group roleplaying Scouts on a camping trip, the rest representing the angry forces of Mother Nature: from a swarm of bees to a grasping, clutching oak tree.

I Don't Know What It Is, But I Know What I Like. One person becomes a modern statue on display, twisting his or her body into a grotesque shape. The rest of the players are spectators trying to figure out the "significance" of this strange and peculiar work of "art."

chapter 3

Reader's Theater

One appealing aspect of a reader's theater production is that it requires very little paraphernalia—no costumes or scenery, little makeup, few props. And although you will need to spend time rehearsing your presentation, you do not need to memorize your lines. Reader's theater is different from a play production in several ways:

- Rather than performing the action of the play, the actor or actors sit or stand facing the audience. The actors use their voices to bring the characters to life, rather than gesture or movement. And the actors communicate directly with the audience instead of with one another.

- Lines need not be memorized. Each actor holds a script and reads from it. However, the actor is familiar enough with the lines that he is able to face the audience most of the time, referring to the script from time to time.

- There is a bare minimum of scenery and props. A backdrop may be made to suggest the mood, the time, or the general locale in which the reading takes place. No costumes are used, but a few props or accessories— a hat, a cane, a pair of eyeglasses—can help emphasize a character. "Street makeup" may be used to highlight features. In formal reader's theater productions, actors and actresses sometimes wear long gowns and suits and ties.

You may want to dress up, but matching or similar clothes—for example, blue jeans and T-shirts—are fine, too.

- Each actor may read the part of more than one character. Actors remain in one place throughout the production, so changes in character must be expressed through changes in the voice. It's possible, then, for three actors to do a play that has six—or even more—characters in it.

- A **narrator** may be used in a reader's theater production to provide information that can't be given by the characters. The narrator can set the scene of the action and give explanations about changes in the setting or the time.

- All kinds of literature may be used as a reader's theater production. Many plays may be read just as they are written. Other plays, as well as comics, stories, parts of novels, and poems may be adapted for reader's theater.

From Page to Play: Reading Plays Aloud

The first step in planning a reader's theater production is the selection of the play you wish to read. You may have a favorite play already in mind. If not, the public or school library has many collections of plays or scenes for young actors and actresses. In selecting the play you wish to use, keep in mind the following:

- Is the play interesting and enjoyable to you? It is not likely that you will be able to read a play with much feeling and conviction unless you like it.

- Who will be in your audience? parents? friends? younger children? Is the play one that they would understand and appreciate?

- Does the play have unique and distinctive **characters**? Is their language vivid and lively? (Remember, it is the language rather than gesture and movement that carries the meaning of the play.)

- Does the play have an interesting **conflict** or problem that is worked out in the course of the play? Will the conflict and its solution capture the attention of the audience?

Adapting the Play. After you have selected the play you wish to use, you may need to make some changes for a reader's theater production. If the play is long, you may wish to shorten it by cutting out some scenes. Work from the **climax** of the play, and add the scenes you will need in order to make the play's action clear to the audience. You will need to write a summary of the events—a **narration**—leading up to the **dialogue** in which the characters begin to speak.

Another concern you will have when you adapt your play for reader's theater is the **stage directions**—information at the beginning of scenes and interspersed throughout the dialogue telling the director, the scene designer, and the actors and actresses how the play should be performed, how the actors should say their lines and move, how the setting should look, what time of day it is, how much time has passed, etc.

Some playwrights provide much more detailed information than others about scenery, action, and actors' delivery. In preparing to adapt your play for reader's theater, you will notice three kinds of stage directions:

• One kind of stage directions tells actors how to say their lines. These appear in parentheses behind the characters' names or are interspersed with the dialogue. The actors and actresses can express these through the use of their voices. For example:

> JUDY: *(desperately)* Give me that ring.
>
> HORACE: *(half coaxing)* Why don't you come and get it?
>
> JUDY: *(her voice rising and now angry)* If you don't give me that ring you'll be very sorry.
>
> MARK: *(groaning)* Will you two kindly stop bickering?
>
> *Edgar enters the room shouting.*
>
> EDGAR: OK, this is a holdup. Give me all your jewelry.

• In reader's theater, some stage directions can be ignored altogether, because the action is not necessary to the meaning of the play. For example:

(She puts the bouquet of flowers in a vase on the table.)

or

(Backing away)

or

(He lies back in the grass with his arms tucked under his head.)

Stage directions such as these give actors information about where and how to move and gesture that add liveliness to the performance, but they are not necessary for the audience's understanding.

• The final type of stage direction is necessary for understanding the play. But this information cannot be communicated by the actor; a narrator's part needs to be added to set the scene, explain significant action, and describe changes in time and place. The following stage directions need to be explained to the audience:

> SCENE 1: *The scene opens in a dark dusty corner of the school library. It looks as if no one has been there in years. There are a few books covered with dust sitting on a small table.* John *enters. He looks around to make sure there is no one else there and then slowly begins to look through the stack of books. Just as he begins to open one,* Eric *comes up behind him and touches his shoulder.* John *jumps and turns.*

or

> (Mark *appears at the window.* John *senses someone there but* Mark *ducks as* John *turns toward him.)*

or

> SCENE 2: *It is two weeks later.* John *sits alone on the steps of the library in the middle of the night. His expression is grim, defeated. He lowers his head and begins to cry silently.*

or

JOHN: I'm going to get out of here. *(He runs to the door and begins to kick it and pound on it. He throws his body against it. Suddenly he sits down and pulls off his shoes. He stands and throws them one after another at the window, shattering the glass.)*

In adapting your play, read through it, marking the stage directions that will need to be read by the narrator. In some cases, the narrator will be able to read them just as they are written. In other instances, the directions will not be written in complete sentences, so they will have to be rewritten.

After you have adapted the play, adding narration for the parts you have left out and for the stage directions, it is time to choose the actors and rehearse the reading.

Reading the Play. Because you won't be using gesture and movement to express yourself in your performance, you must rely on your voice and your ability to read with feeling, force, and the proper emphasis. This is especially true if you are reading the part of more than one character. In order to recreate different characters, you will need to develop variety in your reading and speaking style.

Even though you will be reading from a script, you must *sound* as if you are speaking spontaneously. Read for the ideas, not word for word, emphasizing important words, expressions, feelings.

Here are five ways you can adjust your style of speaking and reading to express different feelings and to create different emphases:

• Use different *rates* of speaking. We usually associate speaking slowly with being relaxed and calm. People who speak *very* slowly are sometimes thought of as lazy or dumb. You can also express tiredness through slow speech. Increase your rate of speaking to express anxiety or nervousness. Fast speech also can be used to show fear or excitement. We also associate fast speech with people who are trying to pull a fast one, so liars and crooks are sometimes portrayed as speaking very fast.

There is a general tendency when you are nervous to speak quickly. This is one thing you will want to concentrate on controlling. Consciously make yourself read slowly, even overemphasizing the slowness for a time to keep yourself from racing through your reading.

• Use different *rhythms* in your speaking. Rhythm refers to the pattern of the accents, the pitch, the rate, and the volume of your speech. For example, some people speak in a monotone. Their voices don't get any higher or any lower in pitch. Some people speak very haltingly. They speak quickly and then they stop; then a few more words come out and then silence. We often can guess what section of the country people come from in part because of the rhythm of their speech. Use a halting rhythm when you are trying to express insecurity on the part of a character; use a steady, even rhythm to express confidence; use a slow singsong rhythm to express boredom.

• Change your *pitch* in speaking. Pitch refers to the highness or lowness of your voice. In general, women's pitches are higher than men's. We often associate very low pitches with tough, rugged cowboys and policemen, and very high pitches with sweet young things. When people are excited they tend to speak not only faster, but higher. People who are angry are sometimes described as "shrill" because their voice gets higher. Use a lower pitch to tell a secret or to express dismay, disappointment, or sadness.

• Change your *volume* in speaking. Some characters have loud, booming voices; others speak quietly because they are reserved or shy or frightened. Show anger and give commands by speaking louder; show close relationships with quiet talk.

• Use *pauses*. Sometimes silence can communicate as much as talk. Avoid the tendency to rush through your play with each line quickly following the previous one. Use pauses to let characters think. Show shock or surprise through a pause. Emphasize an important development in the plot with a pause. Give the audience time to feel an emotional exchange through some silent time. Emphasize important words by pausing just a moment after delivering them.

Rehearsing the Play. Make sure that everyone in the play has a script and has had a chance to read through his or her parts prior to the first rehearsal. Because the actors and actresses will be holding their scripts throughout the performance, the covers should look the same and the pages should be easy to turn. A loose-leaf notebook with rings is probably the easiest to use, but expensive. You might like to make your own covers using construction paper with holes punched in it for rings which can be bought at the dime store.

At the first couple of rehearsals, you will want to accomplish several things: first of all, you will want to be certain that everyone shares the same idea of what the play means and what the characters are like. In some cases it will be clear who are the villains and who are the good guys. But some plays are more complicated and you might need to talk about the play to come to a common interpretation.

Then, read through the play and decide on lines and words to be emphasized. The players might like to mark their scripts to show where there are pauses or they might like to underline words or lines to show emphases. Make sure, too, that everyone knows how to pronounce all the words.

At this point, you should also make certain that the lines you have written for the narrator clarify the action, scenery, and so forth, that is not explained in the dialogue. If you have cut out any of the play, make sure that it moves clearly and smoothly from beginning to end in your new version.

In your next few rehearsals, work on developing the characters. If any actors or actresses are reading more than one part, work on developing the distinction between the two characters. Use the suggestions from the section on *Reading* to create interesting characters. During rehearsals, exaggerate the expression of emotions through the use of various ways of reading your lines. Experiment with different types of voices and emphases and ask your fellow actors and actresses which voices sound best. During the middle rehearsals, all of the characterizations should be refined.

Your final rehearsals will be devoted to polishing your performance.

Even though you have read your lines many times and practiced a great deal, you will need to sound fresh and alive, as though the lines are being uttered spontaneously. Remember, too, to vary the pace and avoid reading the play too fast.

Staging the Play. As we mentioned earlier, the staging requirements of reader's theater are much less elaborate than those of a regular play. Here are some tips on how to stage a reader's theater production.

Arranging the Players. The most important thing in arranging the actors is that you feel and look like a unit. You should not be too far apart, except for the narrator who stands or sits alone to the side. The players may stand or sit, or you may have a combination, with some actors standing and some sitting. Avoid lining up in a straight row. You should stay stationary throughout the performance, though you may move your heads and torsos. Although in reader's theater the players communicate directly with the audience, you need not always face the audience; you can look at one another as it fits the dialogue of the play.

Scenery. Scenery is not required for a reader's theater production. You may wish to have a simple backdrop or curtain to create a mood. Remember that dark colors express a quiet, serious, perhaps even a depressing feeling; light colors express warmth, lightness, and happiness. You may also use simple cardboard cutouts to suggest a place—trees, the skyline of a city, etc. (See also *The Elements of Stagecraft* in Part II.)

Lighting. Again, lighting can be used to establish a mood, and it should be very simple. A crook-neck lamp or two can be used to light up the players—white light bulbs for daytime or happy scenes, green or blue for nighttime or somber scenes. If you use cardboard cutouts, you can place a simple desk light behind them to create a silhouette.

Costumes, Makeup and Props. Keep them simple. No costumes are necessary (and they create problems if any players are doing more than one part), but it is attractive if everyone dresses in similar fashion, say everybody in T-shirts and jeans. Simple props might be used to differentiate among the characters: a professor wearing a pair of glasses, for example, and a baseball player wearing a cap. You might want to use a little makeup to highlight your features, but it should not be used as a means of establishing a character. You can also scatter a few props about the stage to set a mood—baseball bats and gloves for a baseball story; stuffed toys and dolls and a banner or two to represent a girl's room—but do not try to handle or use these props during the production, since your hands will be filled with the script.

Music. You may also use music to set the mood of your performance. Have an appropriate record playing as your audience enters and even very quietly as the narrator begins to speak and set the scene. Music can be used as an interlude between scenes, too. Sound effects can be employed sparingly throughout the reading to highlight the reading. (See also *Radio Plays* in Chapter 5 for ideas on making and using sound effects.)

The Performance. Begin the play by having the narrator introduce it, perhaps saying a bit about why the group selected it and what it is about. The narrator should then introduce the players and the characters they are presenting. It will be helpful to the audience in following the play to know in advance who the characters are.

Some Plays. The best plays for reader's theater are your own, scripted plays, pieces you have written yourself. (We'll discuss writing a play in more detail in the next chapter.) But the young people's section of your library will have collections of plays and skits that you might want to read. A good source of plays are the books published by Plays, Inc. of Boston, including:

Humorous Skits for Young People by Robert Fontaine (1970)
Thirty Plays for Classroom Reading by Donald D. Durrell and B. Alice Crossley (1968)
Plays from Famous Stories and Fairy Tales by Adele Thane (1967)
Plays from Folktales of Africa by Barbara Winther (1976)
Christmas Plays for Young Actors by Abraham Burack (1970)
One Hundred Plays for Children by Abraham Burack (1970)

Fifty Plays for Junior Actors by Sylvia E. Kamerman (1966)
Radio Plays for Young People by Walter Hackett (1950)

Another good collection of funny plays you might look for is Carol Korty's *Silly Soup: Ten Zany Plays* (Scribners, 1977).

Adapting Comics for Reader's Theater

One of the easiest forms of reader's theater for you to produce is the comics, where the conversation is already written out for you in balloons over the characters' heads. All you and your theater troupe need to do is read the lines spoken by the characters, adding facial expressions and gesture to bring the words to life.

Most comics are suitable for reader's theater adaptation, both comic books and the strips in the daily paper. In order to use a cartoon, the point of the cartoon should be communicated through words, rather than pictures. Some *Peanuts* cartoons, for example, cannot be used because the jokes are in the pictures—Lucy pulling away the football so Charlie Brown falls, or Charlie getting his kite stuck in a tree. Although you can invent words so the audience can tell what is happening, it is better to look for comics where the story is conveyed by the dialogue among the characters.

The Short Strip. The comic strip in the Sunday or daily paper is very short, usually from one to ten frames. In most cartoons, you get to know the personality of the characters and the running jokes or gags they use. Garfield, the cat, for example, loves to eat, and so this is a typical exchange:

> MAN: Just look at yourself, Garfield. You're becoming a soft, sugar-dependent, grease-eating lardball. Is that what you want?
> GARFIELD: Yes!
> MAN: Let me rephrase that . . .

In other strips, the gags may not be central to the character's personality. Still other comics, like Doonesbury and Spiderman, are continuing stories.

To create a reader's theater production, begin by collecting your favorite strips, cutting them out of the paper. You may wish to collect one kind of strip, or you might save lots of different ones. Keep in mind that comic strips in the paper are very short, and even those from the Sunday paper take less than a minute to read aloud. You will need to collect quite a few to put together even a ten-minute show.

After you have collected the strips, organize them in some way. If you are using a continuing story, keep it in order as you collect it, so you don't have to reconstruct the plot later. With other cartoons, you can put together strips that are on the same basic idea or theme. Tape them on pieces of paper, leaving room to write in some narration between. Then give your collection a title.

Next write the part for the narrator. The narration should include an introduction to the performance with the title of the show, the names of the characters, and the names of the players. You might also want to include a little on the subject of the show. Then set the scene. Add transitions to explain changes between strips and scenes. If possible, make copies on a photocopy machine for the other players. If that can't be done, have your players hand-copy scripts for their own use (all they need is the words, not the pictures). If you have a music stand or easel around, you can place the script on that so two or three players can share a script.

In putting together a show, you can use the short comic strip in several ways. You might like to do a three-act production with each act a ten-minute collection from a different strip. Or you can use short strips as introductions or interludes between acts of a longer play, entertaining your audience during the breaks. Or you could combine a reader's theater production of a play or a comic book with the reading of some short strips.

The Comic Book. Most comic books include one to three stories and the stories are much longer than newspaper strips. They usually don't rely as much on sight gags, so they are somewhat easier to use. You still need to read through the story you want to use, however, to make certain that the story can be easily told with dialogue. You will need a narrator to introduce the characters and set the scene. Most comic books include "boxes" that give the background and explain the time and place. The narrator should read those boxes. In addition, the narrator will need to provide explanations when the characters do *not* speak, but do something through actions and gestures in the pictures.

Both "funny" books, like *Bugs Bunny, Little LuLu,* and *Archie,* and adventure books—*Spiderman, The Incredible Hulk*—can be adapted for reader's theater, but adventure comics require more adaptation. For example, they are more likely to include "flashbacks," events that occurred *before* the story began and fill in the background. You will need the narrator to explain that the characters are acting out an event that took place earlier. In adventure books a character is often shown alone, thinking about a problem, with those thoughts shown in a squiggly balloon rather than a smooth one. In reader's theater, those thoughts can be presented as a **dramatic monologue,** the character simply thinking aloud to himself or herself. As with plays, thinking can be shown by having the narrator explain that the character is alone or by spotlighting only that character rather than all the players on stage.

With both comic strips and books, it is difficult to know how much narration is needed to make the story clear to your audience. As your troupe rehearses, you may discover places to add more narration. You might also like to read the play to a parent or friend to see if it makes sense to them. Ask for their suggestions or advice before staging the final production.

Adapting Stories

You can also put on a dramatic reading of some of your favorite short stories for an audience, including entertaining younger children by reading some of their favorite children's stories. You will find in doing this that the role of the narrator is greatly expanded. He or she will often need to read longer stretches with descriptions of the actions, the surroundings, the characters, and the thoughts of the characters. Generally, your actors and actresses will read all the parts that fall between quotation marks, and the narrator will read all the rest.

However, it may be possible for you to shorten the story and cut out some unnecessary parts. For example, the narrator probably doesn't need to read every single *he said* or *she said*, for in dramatizing the story, the voices of the actors and actresses will make that clear. You may also want to shorten some stories by cutting out:

- incidents and scenes that are not important to the main action.
- long descriptions of the surroundings.
- long descriptions of how characters look and gesture.

Make copies of the story for every member of the cast and assign parts. Then read slowly through the story, each person with a pencil in hand. You can decide as you read how much to cut and each actor or actress can underline his/her parts to read. Finally, you need to determine if you have to write some new lines for the narrator to clarify any parts of the story.

A story dramatization does not need as much rehearsing as a full-scale play. After a slow reading to mark the parts and a rehearsal or two, you're probably ready to put on a show. Therefore your troupe might like to build a **repertoire,** a collection of stories you can dramatize for different audiences and occasions. There are many short-story collections available in your school or public library that you might like to explore. Consider, for example, the idea of a whole show devoted to:

- science fiction
- mystery
- fantasy
- ghost stories and scary tales
- romance
- myths, fables, legends
- stories for younger kids

In addition, you might like to try a reader's theater adaptation of your favorite *novel*, a full-length story that may run well over one hundred pages. Of course, you probably won't want to read the whole novel, cover to cover. Instead, select some key scenes and climactic episodes that you wish to use. Then write narrator's parts to explain what goes on between these events and fill in the audience on the background.

The One-Person Show

You don't need a group in order to provide entertainment for friends through reader's theater. One-person shows, with actors and actresses playing the parts of such people as American author and humorist Mark Twain or the poet Emily Dickinson, have been popular on the Broadway stage. And the popularity of the "radio reader" programs for adults show that people simply like being read to. (Remember how your parents read to you when you were young? That was a form of reader's theater as well.) Put together a show using some of your favorite pieces of literature—perhaps some of the following.

Stories. A one-person reading of a short story does not have to be adapted. However, you may want to cut the story if it is too long or if it contains parts that you think might not keep your listeners' interest. Keep in mind the audience you will be reading for when you select your story, but make certain it is one you genuinely enjoy. You may want to use fiction (made-up stories) or nonfiction (factual accounts and real-life stories). You can even choose to read a whole book of fiction or nonfiction, either breaking it into installments or selecting the parts you think will most interest your audience.

Rehearse your story before reading it to a live audience. You will want to know the story very well so you can concentrate on your delivery and look at the audience from time to time to gauge their reaction. You might even want to rehearse in front of a mirror. Practice looking up while you read and making facial expressions to go along with what you are reading.

It might also be good to practice once in private with a friend or family member before going on stage for real.

In your performance, remember that the most important thing is to share the literature you are reading with your audience. Give feeling to the author's words, but don't overact, and don't shout. Speak as if you were talking to someone in the back row of your audience. Vary your pace and your manner of delivery. Don't tell the story excitedly throughout or the excitement will lose its impact. Build the ending gradually, alternating intense moments and calm moments. If possible, use a platform to make it easier for your audience to see you. If you do not have anything that will elevate you, leave a bit of space between you and the first row of chairs.

Children's Stories, Nursery Rhymes, and Fairy Tales. Children love to be read to. If you have any younger brothers and sisters, you know the appeal of a story to them. And children's stories are fun to read dramatically. Fairy tales are filled with beauties and beasts and fantastic and sometimes frightening creatures. Mother Goose rhymes are easy to memorize and recite. And the best children's stories and poetry—both old and new—offer charming, funny, fantastic and real worlds that both children and adults enjoy.

In choosing the stories and poems you would like to read, consider the ages of the children you will be reading to. What did you like to read when you were their age? If you have younger children in your family, you can ask them about what they liked at different stages. Find your own childhood favorite books that may have been tucked away in a closet or attic.

Perhaps you would like to volunteer to read to groups of children. Contact the teachers of younger elementary children or of preschoolers or nursery schoolers in your area to see if they would be interested in having you come in to read. Mothers of young children in your neighborhood would probably be very pleased to have you start a story hour for their children. Large libraries often have a children's librarian to conduct story hours, but if your library doesn't, you could start a story hour.

If you are not accustomed to small children, practice reading before small groups before hitting the big time and groups of twenty or more. Children like *drama*. Allow yourself to exaggerate your reading for them, using your voice and movement and gesture to bring the characters and the events of the story to life. If possible, involve the children in the telling of the story. If there is a refrain, let them join in saying it. You may want to stop from time to time during your reading to ask them to tell what they think will happen next. You might even want to teach them to pantomime the actions of the story as you read along, perhaps using the pictures in the book as a guide.

As a final note, remember that if you are reading a picture book, everyone will want to see. Prior to reading, think about where you will stop to show the pictures, making certain that you do not interrupt your own reading.

Poetry. If you are a poetry lover, carry your enthusiasm to others by showing them that poetry is not hard to understand or dull. Though there are some corny poems about love and flowers (there are good ones, too), you can find lively poems about animals, sports, magic, ghosts, holidays, cowboys, computers, and so on. In fact, you can probably find good poems on any topic you can mention. You may already have some favorite poems you'd like to read. If not, you can also find dozens of poetry collections in the library, many of them aimed specifically at young people.

In planning your poetry reading, first decide what your main focus or theme is going to be. You might like to read a number of poems on the same topic, such as:

- Seasons and Celebrations
- Animals (or a specific animal: Dogs, Cats, Horses)
- Earth and Outer Space
- Sports
- Childhood and Growing Up
- People

- Action and Adventure
- Love
- Magic
- The Eerie and Bizarre
- Poems by Young People

Or, you might like to read several poems by the same poet:

• Shel Silverstein writes poetry that is not only humorous and clever, but sometimes thought-provoking. One of his favorites with young people is *Where the Sidewalk Ends*.

• A. A. Milne is best known as the author of the Winnie-the-Pooh stories, but he has also written excellent poetry that you can find in a book, *When We Were Very Young*.

• Nikki Giovanni is well known as a writer of poetry for adults, but she has also written for young people, including a recent collection called *Vacation Time*.

There are many, many other good poets whose poems have been collected. Browse through the library if you don't already have a poet in mind.

Yet another possibility is a reading of poems of a particular type, such as:

Nonsense Poems. A famous writer of nonsense verse is Lewis Carroll, author of *Alice's Adventures in Wonderland*, and you'll find his work collected in *The Humorous Verse of Lewis Carroll* (Dover, 1960). Ogden Nash is a modern humorous poet; look for *Custard and Company* (Little, Brown, 1980) or any of his other books.

Limericks.

There once was a poet named Lear,
Whose limericks were funny to hear.
He wrote quite a bunch.
(You can read them at lunch,
and laugh in your pie and root beer.)

One of Edward Lear's collections is *Limericks by Lear* (World, 1965). Another collector of limericks is Myra Cohn Livingston (*A Lollygag of Limericks*, Atheneum, 1978).

Haiku. This is a Japanese poetry form consisting of three lines and seventeen syllables, usually describing a precise moment or image in nature: an animal eating, a tree in bloom, the sunrise.

Ballads. These are actually songs to be sung, but they can be read or recited effectively in a reader's theater presentation.

You can also do a reader's theater production in which you intersperse poetry and prose. Use a poem as an introduction to a short story, for example. You can also use poems as an interlude between acts of a play, or you could put on a reading of an author who writes both poetry and stories, using excerpts from a variety of his or her works.

In practicing and presenting your poetry to an audience, make use of rhythm and rhyme to communicate the message and feeling of the poem, but don't overemphasize the rhythm and rhyme or make your delivery singsong. Be careful, too, not to drop your voice at the end of each line; read through to the punctuation—the commas, semicolons, and periods— and pause only where there is a punctuation mark. Emphasize words that create the impact and meaning of the poem rather than simply the ones that rhyme. Remember, too, to read the poem slowly and with feeling, without being overly dramatic. During practice sessions, make a tape recording of your reading to hear how it actually sounds and determine what changes to make in your delivery.

When you do your performance, begin with a brief introduction to the entire reading to help people prepare for what is to come. Also use brief introductions before each poem, but don't try to tell your readers what the poem is supposed to mean. You might also want to tell the audience a little about the author's background and life, if you know it. Consider making a tape recording of the actual performance, and if you like the sound of it, mail the tape to a relative or friend.

Dramatic Monologues. In dramatic monologues only one character speaks, addressing an imaginary character or talking to himself or herself. In some monologues, the character pauses as he/she is speaking to "hear" the response of a listener, then resumes speaking. Sometimes dramatic monologues are performed as telephone calls with only one side of the conversation heard by the audience. Other dramatic monologues are created for a speaker who is alone and speaking to himself or to the audience. Robert Browning is a famous author of some poetic dramatic monologues; you may know his "My Last Duchess," in which a speaker describes a portrait of his former wife. William Shakespeare also made use of dramatic monologues—called soliloquies—in his plays; you may be familiar with Hamlet's "To be or not to be" speech.

In the library you will find some books of dramatic monologues created for young people. You might want to look for:

Humorous Monologues for Teen-Agers by Robert Fontaine (Plays, Inc., 1963)

Humorous Monolgues by Vernon Howard (Sterling, 1962)

Modern Monologues for Young People by John Murray (Plays, Inc., 1972)

You can also adapt a story, a scene from a novel, or a scene from a play to create your own monologue. To do this, read the material carefully so you know the story. Then tell it through the eyes, and using the language, of one of the characters.

Letters, Diaries, Memoirs. This kind of reading is a good choice for a one-person show because it is a person's reflections about his or her life. On stage you can become a famous historical person, a political leader, a scientist or explorer, an artist, painter, singer, or composer. You can talk directly to the audience in "your" (the author's) own words about "your" life and feelings. Search the card catalogue at the library to find books written by your favorite famous people. Find portions of their lives that you think are especially moving or interesting. If you take excerpts from a book or letter, make certain you explain to your audience what went on beforehand, or where this event falls in the person's life. You might also like to explain to the audience why you chose to read this person's writing and why he or she is significant to you.

Reading Your Own Writing

If you like to write, either in school or on your own, you may have a drawerful of manuscripts that nobody but you has ever read. Consider presenting your work in a reader's theater production. Or, if you like to write, or think you'd like to write, but don't have any manuscripts on hand, write something that you intend to present in reader's theater. If you feel a bit nervous about presenting your *own* writing, or if you think people would believe you are egotistical, take a pen name for the night and read your own stuff as if it were written by somebody else. (If the audience claps loud and long, you may want to reveal your true identity as the author.) Some of the things you can write and read include:

• poems of all kinds . . . poems about your experiences and feelings, your observations of the world, your philosophical thoughts, your friends and family.

• stories . . . either real or imaginary, true experiences or fantastic adventures.

• letters and diaries . . . some that you have actually written describing events in your life, or a series of fictional letters and made-up diary entries about another person.

• jokes and funny stories . . . either ones you've heard or those you've written especially for this occasion.

In presenting your writing, there are three ways to highlight your work:

1. *The Montage.* Here you include your own writing in a reader's theater production of many people's work. For example, weave in some of your poems about cats along with Ogden Nash's humorous observations. Or read

one of your children's stories at a nursery school along with a story by Dr. Seuss or A. A. Milne.

2. *Writers' Showcase*. Get together with other people who like to write and plan a production. You can read and discuss each other's writing and make suggestions for improvement, encouraging one another as you polish and refine your work. Eventually, decide which pieces of writing you want to use and the order you want them in. Readers can introduce themselves to the audience or you can have a master or mistress of ceremonies to handle that. Often people in the audience would like to know where the idea for a story or poem came from, so build in discussion time after the presentation. Perform your Writers' Showcase for friends, neighbors, schools, churches, retirement communities. Pick up new members of the group—adults, perhaps, as well as other kids—as you go along. Perhaps you can make Writers' Showcase a permanent part of your community.

3. *One-Person Reading*. Perhaps you are a writer with a whole sheaf of writing. Put together a show using just your own works and entitle it The Unpublished Works of (your name) or, The Heretofore Unheard Works of_____. Intersperse the reading of your poems and stories with information about where you got your ideas, when and where you started writing, what your favorite pieces are. As a special treat, run off copies of one of your particular favorites for members of the audience to take with them.

chapter **4**

Creating Your Own Play

If you have not written a play, you will find it somewhat different from writing a story. There is no narrator or storyteller in a play. Therefore, you cannot describe for the audience what people look like, what the surroundings are like, or what people are thinking or feeling. You cannot tell the audience what you—the author—think or believe. Everything the audience discovers must come from the dialogue—what the characters say—and from the appearance of the sets and players. Although both stories and plays have a conflict or a problem to be solved, drama emphasizes conflict.

In this chapter we will give you some suggestions on how to write a play—where to get your ideas, how to create conflict, how to develop characters, how to write dialogue, and how to write useful stage directions.

Ideas for Plays

In the following pages we will suggest some starting points for plays. Some ideas might be good for short mini-dramas; some will work for longer, one-act plays; and still others are complex enough for a play of two or three acts. You might like to begin to keep a writer's notebook with ideas for plays: interesting events you observe, snatches of conversation you overhear, captivating people you see, ideas you get from reading or watching

TV or movies. To begin your notebook you might jot down some of these ideas:

Your Own Experiences. Events and people that have had a strong impact on you or that you have remembered for a long time are good starting points for creating plays. In writing your drama, you may stick very closely to the real incident, or you may change things—the names and sexes of the characters, the time and place that it occurred, the number of people involved, and so forth.

- Embarrassing Experiences: getting lost at a new school; forgetting to show up for a friend's birthday party or a baby-sitting job; telling a secret your parents told you not to; eating the candy your sister got for your mom's Mother's Day present; getting caught in a lie.
- Mistakes: cheating on a test; lying to your grandmother; taking something that did not belong to you; breaking or losing something valuable.
- Conflicts: fighting with your parents about your friends, your allowance, your homework or grades, your household chores; fighting with your sisters and brothers or friends about revealing secrets, cheating at games, being friends with their enemies, telling on them.
- Surprises: getting unexpected birthday presents, visits, long-distance phone calls, short-distance phone calls; winning a contest; getting an award.
- Disappointments: losing an important game; losing something special to you; losing a friend through a fight; moving away; getting a bad grade; failing a test; disappointing your parents or teacher; getting accused of something you did not do.
- Disasters: the car breaking down in the middle of nowhere; the washing machine overflowing; accidentally mowing down your neighbors' flowers; forgetting your music in the middle of a piano recital or your lines in the middle of a play performance; dropping your mother's birthday cake in the middle of singing "Happy Birthday."
- Frightening Situations: getting lost in the grocery store, the baseball stadium, the zoo; being left alone at night for the first time and hearing strange noises; being approached by a scary-looking stranger on the street;

riding a horse for the first time; going to the dentist to get your braces put on.

• Painful Experiences: having a serious illness or injury; illness or injury of a friend or family member; losing a loved one through death; losing a pet.

Made-Up Situations and Characters. Even when you are writing plays from your own imagination or are "borrowing" characters or ideas from books, TV, or movies, your own experiences will be the basis of what you write. Your unique ideas and individual viewpoint is important in creating interesting characters and involving situations. Even TV writers, confined by the program they are writing for, need to be original in their writing. Try giving new life to cops, kings, doctors, lawyers, witches, Texans, Martians, and mothers when you create your play. Use . . .

Television Shows and Movies: Think of a new twist when you create an episode for your favorite TV show or movie. Use the characters that are already in the program, creating an episode that fits with their personalities. But put them in a new situation and add some new characters that will show some new aspects to an old story for . . .

    . . . detective and police shows
    . . . lawyer and judge shows
    . . . doctor and nurse shows
    . . . single parents and stepparents
    . . . large families
    . . . rich families
    . . . poor-but-happy families

Develop a new TV show, a situation comedy about people who . . .

    . . . run a circus
    . . . train bears or pigs
    . . . play in a bagpipe band
    . . . teach ballet

. . . run a preschool

. . . tend beehives

. . . lay carpet

What are their problems likely to be? What kinds of people are likely to be a part of their lives? What do they do for fun?

Or, write a drama entitled . . .

. . . Peoria

. . . Big Springs

. . . Castle Butte

. . . Riverside

. . . Kalamazoo

. . . Lakeview

. . . Your Own Hometown

What do the names of the towns suggest about the lives and experiences of the people who live there? What is unique about your own town? Can you create a drama with the lives of some of the people you know who live there?

Fantasy Worlds: Create a world in which things happen as you want them to, like . . .

. . . The Future: What will people eat? Where will they live? How will they dress? What kind of transportation will they have? What will the government be like? the schools? entertainment? religion? What sorts of problems will humans have?

. . . Other Galaxies: Is there life on other planets? What sort? Are they friendly? frightening? fierce? How do they live? What do they look like? What problems are they facing?

. . . Underground Worlds: Who lives underground? Who lives in the center of the earth? Are they shy? bold? invisible? Do they visit the top of the earth? How do they spend their time? Do they like people? What are their problems?

... Underwater Worlds: Who lives there? Anything besides fish and sharks? What is in those sunken ships that have never been found? Why haven't they been found?

... Animal Worlds: Stuffed animals come to life in *Winnie-the-Pooh* and real animals lead secret lives in Beatrix Potter's Peter Rabbit stories. What do you think stuffed animals do while you sleep? Does your cat lead a secret life?

... Favorite Fantasies: Create your own version of the lives of elves, fairies, witches, goblins, ghosts, and hobbits. What problems do they face in a world overpopulated by humans?

Historical Worlds: Learn about an historical era, event, or figure and write a drama about this. Stay true to the real-life events and make guesses about what happened behind the scenes. Or, recreate history according to your own liking. Some possibilities . . .

... The Civil War
... The French, American, Russian Revolutions
... The Pilgrims
... The Age of Arthur
... The Lewis and Clark Western Expedition
... Florence Nightingale
... The Wright Brothers and the Birth of Flight
... The Building of the Egyptian Pyramids
... Queen Elizabeth
... Michelangelo

Foreign Worlds: Learn about another country and set a drama there. Have the play reveal the life-style and problems of the people in the place you have picked . . .

... China
... Mexico
... Malaysia

. . . Egypt
. . . Italy
. . . England
. . . Zimbabwe
. . . Brazil

A Value or Belief: Base a play on a belief that you have. Begin by making a list of things you think are true or should be true and then create a situation and some characters to illustrate your point. Some of your beliefs might be in the form of famous sayings or aphorisms, such as these:

Cheaters never win.
Beauty is only skin deep.
Love conquers all.
It is better to be safe than sorry.
Better late than never.
A penny saved is a penny earned.
It is better to give than to receive.
Laugh and the world laughs with you; cry and you cry alone.
A bird in the hand is worth two in the bush.
A rolling stone gathers no moss.
Man does not live by bread alone.
Too many cooks spoil the broth.
It is better to have loved and lost than never to have loved at all.
Two heads are better than one.

Or, you may make a list of some of your beliefs, observations, or values that you have learned from your own experience:

Cheaters sometimes win.
A friend is the most important thing in the world.
Working with friends is better than working alone.
The new kid in school always has a rough time.
The new kid in school gets most of the attention.

Sometimes people put their trust in the wrong people.
Wealth doesn't always bring happiness.
It is better to be smart than beautiful.
It is better to be beautiful than smart.
You have to pay a price to be popular.
Parents do not understand their kids.
Kids today are spoiled.
Kids mature very early nowadays.
Kids are smarter than their parents.

The Conflict

After you have settled on the idea you would like to use for your play, you will need to decide on the central conflict or problem of the play. Your main character or characters can have conflicts with other people, conflicts within themselves, or problems because of a circumstance they are in or an event that occurs. Here are some problems characters might find themselves facing:

• A family is planning a vacation. Mom and Dad want to go to the big city to enjoy museums, restaurants, and plays. The kids want to go to Disney World. Who will win and how will the problem be resolved?

• Martin tells his parents he is going to a friend's house for the evening. Later that night, his sister catches him at the House of Woogie, the electronic game center. If she tells their parents, he will be grounded, and, more important, his parents will lose their trust in him. Should Martin confess, try to shut his sister up, or deny it all? How will the family members feel about one another in the end?

• HoJo, the moblock, is curious. He is tired of living underground and wants to see what life among humans is like. He ventures off to visit a wonderful place he has heard of—Chicago. But once he gets there he is lost and bewildered and wants to go back home. How will he find his way? Who will he encounter? Will they help him or . . . ?

In writing your play, think about it in three parts:

In the first part, you introduce your main characters and hint at or introduce the problem that they will encounter. You should arouse your audience's curiosity and make them wonder about what is going to happen.

In the second part, you show how the problem develops and then leads to the crisis or the conflict that the characters need to solve.

In the third part, the characters take action so that the problem is resolved. Take Jackson, for example:

The opening: As the play begins, Jackson Alexander has moved to a new community just before the first day of school. He will be going to a huge junior high. He has not made any friends yet, and he does not know his way around. He wants to make a good impression and is terribly afraid of making a fool of himself.

The crisis: Sure enough, Jackson does get lost. He is embarrassed to ask where the cafeteria (or the boys' bathroom, or the bandroom) is. All the other kids seem so self-confident, and all of them already have friends. Jackson finally gets up his nerve to ask and he is laughed at.

The solution: Jackson's mother calls a new friend who has a son Jackson's age who agrees to show Jackson around for the next few days.

or

Jackson secretly follows another student who has the same schedule. The kid figures out what is going on and Jackson makes a friend.

or

Jackson gets into a fight with the kids who laughed at him. Both boys are taken to the principal's office and Jackson's misery is uncovered.

It is important to hint at the crisis as soon as the play opens, so that you can grab your audience's attention. Include some mini-crises as you are going along, so that the audience will remain involved with the emotions of your characters. For example, in the story of Jackson, you could have him fighting with his parents about the move and refusing to go to school, to show the strength of his doubts. You could also include a part where he is trying to make a good impression at school and does something embarrassing. Make sure that it is clear to the audience *why* the problems occur. And make sure that the solution happens in a believable way. Don't grab a solution out of a hat.

It is a good idea to know where your play is going before you begin it. Decide in advance what the central crisis is going to be and how you are going to solve the crisis. Occasionally you will have some interesting characters in mind but not know for sure what is going to happen to them. As you write, a problem should occur to you. If it doesn't, you probably do not have the makings for a play.

The Characters

Make your characters unique individuals with interesting problems and a range of feelings. Don't use the same old stereotypes: the macho football player with no brains, the prissy English teacher who never has a comma out of place, the long-haired drummer always on drugs. Give the characters different aspects to their personalities: perhaps the football player teaches chess at the YMCA; and the English teacher works on a Mississippi riverboat during the summers; and the drummer is the head of the sociology department at the local university. And they have all suffered disappointments, losses, rejections. And they have unique goals and hopes and plans. On the surface your characters may seem to be "types." But as they talk and react to the situation they are in, the audience will discover new things about them.

Create characters that your audience will care about and that *you* care about. You want your audience's reaction to be definite, not wishy-washy, whether they like, dislike, fear, or laugh at a character.

Make your characters distinguishable from one another. Even two brothers, a husband and a wife, two high-school biology teachers, and two ballet dancers will have different personalities, ideas, and responses to their surroundings. Your characters should respond in different ways to the events and crises in the play.

Before you begin to write your play, you should know your main characters quite well—their likes and dislikes, their goals, their beliefs. When characters act and speak they will do it on the basis of these things. Your characters' actions should be motivated, which means they should do what they do for a reason. Characters' actions should not happen "out of the blue" but should be what we might expect those people to do.

Some of your characters will be very much like you in their ideas and opinions. Others will be based on people you have known. Try creating characters putting together combinations of traits of people you have known.

You will create your characters through the use of dialogue or the way they talk and through their actions and appearance, which are described in the stage directions. We will discuss these in the next two sections.

The Dialogue

In Chapter 1, Warm-Ups, we suggested that you listen to the different ways people talk and try imitating them in order to create believable characters. In a play, so much is communicated to the audience through dialogue that the playwright has to have a good ear for speech in order to be successful. In addition to creating the conflict and moving the plot, the dialogue characterizes the people in the play. Characters reveal their values, ideas, and feelings, as well as their educational, geographical, social, and occupational backgrounds. The audience learns about the character through what he or she says and how he or she says it.

Before writing a play, do a lot of listening to the way people talk. Try to eavesdrop in a variety of places so that you can hear different kinds of people talk: rich people and poor people; people from a variety of jobs—storekeepers, bricklayers, bus drivers, college students, bankers, repairmen; people from different parts of the country; people from different racial and ethnic backgrounds. Notice the difference in the way your two parents talk. How is your English teacher's language different from your biology teacher's? What are some interesting features about your doctor's speech?

Notice the differences in people's—

• pronunciation or accent. People from different parts of the country or from different countries have accents that are the most noticeable. Sometimes poets and novelists try to represent these "dialects" by the way they spell the words. For example, they might use "yer" for "you," "kin" for "can," "ol' " for "old," "lyin' " for "lying." If the way one of your characters pronounces something is important, then you can respell the word so it looks the way you want it pronounced.

• usage. Some people say, "I ain't going" and some say, "I'm not going." Some say, "I didn't bring my coat" and some say, "I didn't bring no coat." Some say, "He don't know" and some, "He doesn't know." Listen for other differences in grammatical usage that you might use to help characterize your people.

• word choices. Do you say "soda" or "pop"? "sack" or "bag"? "swear" or "cuss"? Do you call your father "Dad" or "Pa" or "Pop"? Do you shop at the "store" or the "market"? Pay attention to the different words people use and they will enrich your dialogue.

Notice, too, how people express their emotions. Listen for expressions of anger, joy, grief, excitement, irritation. Collect greetings and leave-takings. What can characters say besides "hello" and "good-bye"? How do different people ask for help or service at a restaurant or store or ticket counter? How do people admit they are wrong or apologize?

Listening to other people talk will give you ideas for how to make your character seem real and believable through the way he or she talks. Be careful when you are eavesdropping, however, not to tune in on conversations that are intended to be private (though undoubtedly you would learn a great deal about how people use language!). Listen to people in checkout lines, elevators, football games, the school cafeteria, the classroom, and other public places where they are obviously not intending to keep a secret. Avoid putting your ears against keyholes and furnace registers.

One important thing to remember in writing your dialogue is that although it seems like regular conversation, it is not the same as conversation. Real people talk in circles, repeat themselves, have trouble finding the right word, hem and haw ("uh, I meant to say . . . um, well . . ."), and use clichés or worn-out expressions. Although you want your dialogue to *sound* natural, you also want it to be more direct and to the point. You do not want your characters to get off the subject, like people do in real life. Nor do you want them to use clichés, such as "I'm so hungry I could eat a horse" or "He was as mad as a hornet" or "She looks as pretty as a picture." You want to draw on what you have learned about the way people talk, but you want your dialogue to sound fresh and lively at the same time.

Make sure your characters speak differently from one another, too. The characters can be easily distinguished when you have a teenager and a grandparent or a bank robber and a lawyer or a hairdresser and a truck driver speaking to one another. But two teenagers should speak differently from one another; so should two doctors, two parents, two teachers. When you are writing your dialogue, then, make sure that two (or more) distinct characters are speaking.

Your dialogue is also the means by which you give the audience new information. When a new character enters the scene, you may need to give the audience information about his or her background. Or you may have to let the audience know why a place has sentimental value for a husband and wife. Or you may have to explain why everyone is afraid of the biology teacher.

In a novel, the storyteller could simply give the information through a flashback or even an explanation. In a play, the characters have to provide the information. Try to weave it in naturally, with characters asking questions or remembering incidents that are in keeping with what is happening at the present.

Stage Directions

The stage directions are provided by the playwright so that the actors and actresses, the director, and the scene designer know how to stage the play. They include information about how the performers should move, speak, gesture, feel, and appear. In addition, they describe the scenery, the costumes, and the props needed for the play.

At the beginning of the play, there is usually a page listing all of the characters and telling something about them. For example:

Laura Anderson, a fifteen-year-old girl
Alexandra Anderson, her twelve-year-old sister
David Anderson, their father
Mary Anderson, their mother
The Policeman
The Jeweler
Todd, Laura's boyfriend

The first page of the play also gives an overview of the play summarizing each act or scene. A one-act play might look like this:

Time: The present

SCENES

SCENE I: The Anderson's living room, 8:00 PM, Saturday,
SCENE II: The jewelry store, two days later.
SCENE III: The Anderson's living room, that night.

At the opening of each scene, there is a description of the setting and of the people who are on the stage as the play begins:

SCENE I

(The living room of the Andersons'. It is a comfortable room that shows signs of a lively household. A coffee table with a game board and game pieces sits in front of a couch, center

stage. A desk, stage left, is covered with several open books. Stage right is a large comfortable chair with an end table and lamp next to it. A basket with yarn and knitting needles overflowing from it is in the chair. The door to the outside is behind the couch; stage left is the door to the bedrooms; stage right is the door to the kitchen.

Laura enters stage left. She is an attractive, peppy, happy girl, obviously dressed to go out, in bright, stylish clothes. She begins looking around the room and searches the desk, the coffee table, the end table and yarn basket, picking things up and moving them around. She stands straight abruptly and turns toward the kitchen.)

LAURA: *(whining)* Mother!

Descriptions of the scenes should tell the players' troupe and the audience a great deal about the people who are in the play.

Stage directions continue throughout the dialogue of the play. Sometimes they are given in parentheses preceding the character's dialogue. Other times they are between characters' speeches. They tell the actors and director various things:

• Stage directions tell when characters enter and exit and which direction. They also describe what the characters are wearing or carrying and how they look.

(Mary enters stage right. She is carrying a wine glass in one hand and a cracker in the other. She is a young-looking, attractive forty-year-old wearing blue jeans and western shirt. She moves downstage toward her daughter.)

MARY: Yes, dear.

or

(Laura exits stage left, wailing. Alexandra stomps out the front door. David and Mary sink into the couch together.)

- Stage directions describe gesture, facial expressions, and movement.

> MARY: *(moving away)* What are we going to do about them?
> DAVID: *(following her)* Just don't worry about them so much.
> MARY: *(turning toward him and frowning)* Maybe you should worry about them a little more.
> DAVID: *(shaking his finger at her)* You do it enough for both of us.

- Stage directions describe how characters speak.

> LAURA: *(angrily)* How often have I told you to stay out of my stuff?
> ALEXANDRA: *(softly)* It was an accident.
> LAURA: *(shouting)* An accident? How could someone get into a jewelry box by accident?
> TODD: *(coaxingly while touching Laura's shoulder)* Laura, why don't you just forget it. I'll buy you another pearl.
> LAURA: *(turning toward Todd; coldly)* You keep out of this. Alexandra has bugged me once too often.

To help your players know where to move, you might want to include a diagram which shows the meaning of upstage, downstage, L, C, and R. Upstage means away from the audience; downstage means toward the audience; C means center. Right and left refer to the actor or actresses directions as he or she *faces* the audience. DR, then, means downstage right and DL means downstage left, and so forth. (See more on this in Part II.)

It is also helpful to the troupe to have a list of props somewhere in the script. You might even want to divide them by scene. For example:

Properties: SCENE I: game board and game pieces, basket with knitting needles and yarn, several books, wine glass, box of crackers, several pieces of jewelry—rings, bracelets, necklaces. SCENE II: a glass case or a frame made of wood that looks like a glass case, several pieces of jewelry of different types, a small box, a small paper bag. SCENE III: same as Scene I with addition of small box and small paper bag, bouquet of flowers.

The descriptions of furniture and setting will appear at the beginning of each scene.

The important thing to remember in writing stage directions for your play is that their purpose is to help the actors, director, and production crew stage the play that you have written. Make your stage directions clear, direct, and to the point.

Mini-Dramas

A good way to practice writing complete scripts is to create a very short play, a mini-drama that may last just a minute or two, with a script two or three pages long. If a minute seems to you like an impossibly short time for a play, take a look at some of the mini-dramas that are presented as television commercials. In a single thirty-second or one-minute commercial, an advertiser can often provide a little skit with several characters and still have time left over to tell you about the glories of the product being sold.

A mini-drama should have just one scene, and the action must unfold rapidly. In planning your drama, pick a moment in which your characters are in conflict, a moment in which a quick decision must be made or a tight spot gotten out of.

Here are some ideas for mini-dramas:

• Jan's friends are leaving for the movies now, but her mom says she has to do the dishes before she can leave the house. Something's gotta give.

• The coach tells Eric that if he wants to play basketball, he cannot play football. Eric wants to talk him out of it.

• Joe has just discovered he's on the wrong bus, an express bus across town. He's at the back, the bus is packed, and the bus driver is a stickler for rules.

• Richard and the palace guard are waiting outside the arena for Richard to go and fight the lion. Richard would really like to get out of this one. Is there any escape?

• Suzy has just been discovered in her big sister's room, playing with her big sister's jewelry box, by her big sister.

• The vet says John's cat will never recover. Should John take his beloved cat home anyway or should he have the vet put it to sleep?

• Ed has just asked Alice to the prom. She really wants to go with Tony, but he hasn't asked her yet. She'd hate to be stuck at home.

Use the procedures suggested for scriptwriting earlier in this chapter in writing your mini-drama. Here are some guidelines that are particularly important for a very short play:

1. Have your characters introduce one another by name and present the basic problem in their opening lines. For example, the scene with Eric and his coach might begin this way:

> COACH: *(sadly)* Eric, you know you are a heck of a football player and I would sure hate to lose you.
>
> ERIC: *(surprised)* What do you mean, coach? You know I love football and I don't plan to ever give up the game.
>
> COACH: *(thumping Eric on the back)* I'm glad to hear you say that boy, cuz there's something I've been meaning to talk to you about.

2. Get your characters involved in a conflict or problem right away. In the example above, there is a hint of a problem in the very first line and the next two arouse the audience's interest about what the problem is going to be. In this scene, the problem is presented in the opening line:

> MARTHA: *(shouting)* Suzy! Just what are you doing in my jewelry box?

3. Have your play move toward a conclusion promptly. In the scene with Eric and the coach, for instance, 1) Eric might listen to the coach's reasons calmly and decide to quit football, 2) Eric might decide that the coach is off-base and leave the football team in anger, 3) the coach might be angry about Eric's hesitance to quit basketball and threaten to get him kicked off

both teams. In the scene with the jewelry box, 1) Suzy might come up with a really good explanation of why she's in the jewelry box, 2) Martha might call her mother, who punishes Suzy, 3) Martha might get into a huge fight with Suzy, bringing their mother's wrath and punishment down on both of them. No matter how you end, it is important that you draw your play firmly to a close.

Make a list of some "what if" situations as starting points for mini-dramas. What if:

- the teacher accused Sally of something she did not do.
- Mark's parents are not home when a person comes to the door claiming to be an old friend of Mark's father.
- Kelly's baby-sitter wants to invite her boyfriend in when the parents have expressly forbidden it.
- Toby's dad has just run over Toby's bike and has to tell him about it.
- Two hikers claim they have found a pot of gold at the end of the rainbow, but they cannot get the people in town to believe them.

Grab a pen and start writing mini-drama. Use one of our ideas or a "what if" of your own. When you are finished, round up a crew of actors and actresses and ask them to perform your play. *Idea:* Write several mini-dramas and present them as an afternoon or evening entertainment for family, friends, neighbors, or classmates.

The One-Act Play

The one-act play might have a fairly simple conflict or problem that needs to be solved, but you take more time solving it. The one-act play can have two, three, or more scenes, so that the character is shown not just at the moment he or she recognizes the problem, but at the first hint of the problem, the crisis point, and after the crisis is over.

Any of the problems we suggested in the Mini-Dramas section can be used as a one-act play. Take, for example, the story of John who discovers that his cat is terminally ill:

SCENE I: John's house. John notices that his cat is acting funny. He consults with his mother, who agrees and suggests that John take the cat to the vet. John frets and worries about the seriousness of the illness.

SCENE II: The vet's office, several hours later. The vet tells John that the cat has a rare form of leukemia. He says the cat will not survive long and that it is suffering some pain. He tells John that he may take the cat home if he wishes or he may have it put to sleep.

SCENE III: John's house, several days later. The audience learns that John's cat was put to sleep and that John allowed it to be studied for science. John reads a letter to his family from the vet that says that John's cat helped scientists come up with some important findings about the rare disease.

Keep the changes in scenes in your one-act play very simple. Because the play is short, you do not want to disrupt the mood or spend too much time changing scenery. Two or three quick changes in a half-hour show is ample. Likewise, limit your cast of characters. The audience does not have enough time to identify and become familiar with a large number of people in a short play.

Plays with More Than One Act

The two- or three-act play can involve a much more complex problem and a more difficult solution than the mini-drama or the one-act play. There are some other differences:

1. There may be more scenes, more changes in place in the long play than the one-act play. Because the two- or three-act play takes longer to perform, breaks to change the set do not seem so disruptive. (Some long plays *do* have the same setting throughout.)

2. The long play may occur over a much longer period of time—several days, several weeks, even several years. (Or, if you wish, the action can take place in a period of hours.)

3. In a longer play, the writer is able to create characters with much more depth. The main characters usually change and grow during the course of the play.

4. There may be several crises in a longer play, rather than just one conflict. You set up a problem, create a solution, only to introduce another, unexpected problem which ruins everything again. Take the Walt Disney version of *Cinderella*, for example.

- Problem: Cinderella wants to go to the ball, but she has no gown, no materials to make one, and no time to make one since she has to wait hand and foot on her stepmother and stepsisters.
- Solution: Cinderella's animal friends make a ball gown for her.
- New Problem: Cinderella's mean stepsisters are jealous of her beauty and tear her new ball gown to shreds.
- Another Solution: Cinderella's Fairy Godmother fixes her up and sends her off beautifully attired to the arms of the Prince.
- Yet Another Problem: Just as the Prince and Cinderella fall in love, the clock strikes twelve and Cinderella must leave the ball without telling the Prince who she is or where to find her.
- A Possible Solution?: The Prince finds her glass slipper and vows to find her.
- Alas, Another Problem: Cinderella's stepsisters lock her in her room where she is unable to try on the slipper.
- The Final Solution: The mice friends let Cinderella out, the slipper fits, and Cinderella is taken to the Prince to become his bride.

In planning and writing your play with more than one act, think of situations that lead to problems. The problems can be amusing, frightening, complicated, or sad. Think of the people who might encounter problems, and the various ways they might solve their problems. Do not use the most obvious or easiest solution. In fact, sometimes create "solutions" that only complicate the problems or lead to more trouble.

Here are some situations to get you started thinking about the problems people face. Add more of your own:

• Joe Andrews has finally made starting pitcher. On the day of the biggest game of the season he breaks his finger. But he just *has* to pitch anyway.

• A local girl, Ann Czynk, agrees to marry the prince of Alakuluha Island. She has no idea what she is letting herself in for.

• Dewey Oxford gets caught copying answers during his final exam. No one can understand why such a good student would have to do such a thing.

• Terry Dellinger discovers outer space creatures that make themselves visible only to him. Who will believe him?

• Cathy and Maureen are best friends until they both feel that they should have the lead in the school play.

chapter 5

Media Plays

Although drama is as old as recorded history, going back thousands and thousands of years, one kind of playmaking is relatively new—less than one hundred years old. That drama is *media plays*, the subject of this chapter. The **media** for our purposes simply means ways of transmitting a play to an audience that is some distance from the actors and actresses, and we'll discuss three major forms of media that you're already quite familiar with: *radio, television*, and *film*. Now it may seem a little farfetched for you to think of writing for the movies or prime-time television (though young people *have* done it successfully), and the odds are against your selling a script, say, to a major television network. But you can, right in your own neighborhood, do some variations of commercial media plays—using tape recorders, for instance, to make a radio broadcast, or perhaps doing a television program using a videotape recorder owned by your school or somebody's parents. You may also be surprised to learn that you can find audiences—real audiences—for some of your media productions right around your neighborhood, actually getting some of your tapes and films played on television or radio stations. We'll show you how.

Radio Plays

Return with us now to the thrilling days of yesteryear, when out of a tall wooden box filled with glowing tubes floated the sounds of static and the voices of actors and actresses bringing thrilling radio plays; when the Lone Ranger and his Indian friend Tonto prowled the airwaves making the West a safe place to live and Sergeant Preston and his team of huskies did the same for the Yukon Territory; when "The Soaps" meant fifteen-minute radio plays, done live from a studio in New York, rather than videotaped sagas filling in the gaps between commercials and game shows.

Chances are you're too young to remember the era of radio drama, but for about forty years before television became popular, the radio provided the central form of media entertainment in America, serving far more people than the movies. In the 1950's, when television sets became reasonably priced and there was one in every neighborhood, if not every house, radio drama disappeared, and radio stations, trying to keep their listeners, shifted over to a news-and-music format. As kids, we were sorry to see radio drama go. In our minds, no TV superhero in his living-color costume can be quite so exciting as The Shadow, a hero of radio drama, an ordinary man who had the ability "to cloud men's minds" and make himself seem invisible, who spoke in a spooky whisper.

But we don't want to become nostalgic, because radio drama is alive in the hearts and minds of many young playmakers, and after reading this section, perhaps you'll want to join them.

The advantage of radio plays is that they do not require any **sets** or **props.** A radio play can take place anywhere: the Wild West, on the planet Xanthophyl, on the head of a pin, in the human bloodstream. All you have to do is ask your readers to imagine the place. Thus, while movies and films often need to be made "on location," a radio play can be tape-recorded any old place, maybe even in a closet.

Further, radio allows your actors and actresses to extend the range of their talents and become believable as new characters. Let's face it: an eleven-year-old or thirteen-year-old portraying an adult on the stage or on television or film still often looks his or her age. Not so on radio, where you can take on many different roles successfully. (In fact, if you can change your voice or your dialect, you can often play several roles in a radio drama.) Thus with even a small cast, you can do incredible things, including transforming yourselves into the entire crew of the Starship Enterprise.

The disadvantage of radio drama, one that presents a great challenge to the scriptwriter, is the fact that you have no images or pictures to work with. Thus the language of your play must be very sharp and precise. Your characters can't wave their arms on radio to get a point across; they can't scowl silently to intimidate or frighten an enemy. If they do, the radio simply goes silent and nobody knows what is happening.

To make up for the lack of pictures, radio scriptwriters use a variety of techniques and strategies that you may want to draw upon in your own work:

Writing Visually. Whenever you want your listeners to get a clear picture in their minds, weave in a description of the scene or a character's appearance. For example:

> ROBERTA: Hey, Bob, I like that pink shirt. The red stripes on the collar make it flashy.
>
> ROBERT: Thanks, Bobbie, I got it specially to go with my maroon checked slacks.

Using Dialogue to Describe Action. If it is not clear to a listener what is happening in a scene, have your characters talk about it:

> TOM: Don't look now, but I think your horse is going to finish last; it's fourteen lengths out of the lead and losing ground fast.
>
> TINA: I'm not giving up hope yet! I think he's going to gain on that big chestnut horse that's in next-to-last place.

Introducing the Narrator. Some stage plays have **narrators** who help to explain the action to an audience. In a radio play, the narrator may be essential. For example, frequently the narrator will introduce a scene, tell about the setting, and even catch the listeners up on the action to date:

> NARRATOR: In our last episode, Frank and Nancy, our intrepid teen-age detectives, snooped once too often and were captured by that archvillain, Dr. Evil, who has locked them in his coal cellar. Now, as rats run across their feet and spiders make webs in their hair, our heroine and hero discuss their future—such as it is.

The narrator will also speak during the radio play, sometimes changing the scene:

> NARRATOR: Meanwhile, back at the ranch.

or describing something that happens:

> NARRATOR: Suddenly, Frank clasped his hand to his chest in pain.

Using Sound Effects. This is the fun part of radio drama as far as we're concerned. To let listeners know what is happening, the scriptwriter can build in sound effects. A door opens, creaking on its hinges to set up a scene. A dog howls in the distance. Footsteps clatter down an empty hall as the hero runs toward or away from something. (We'll have more to say about how to create sound effects in the next section.)

Using Background Music. You are familiar with the ways in which music is used on television and in film to create a mood—slow, sad music for a death scene; fast music with xylophones for chases; organ music to create suspense. Actually, that convention began with radio plays, where music was used to provide the listener with clues as to what was happening. Music can also be used as a substitute for a *curtain*, and you can introduce music to signal that a scene has ended or to bridge the gap between one scene and another.

Ideas for Radio Plays. In Chapter 2 we presented a number of ideas for improvised plays "made up as you go along." Many of those ideas of scenes for one, two, three or more people will also work for radio, so begin by scanning the ideas presented in that chapter before considering such ideas as:

Radio Adventures. Some of the heroes and heroines of old-time radio drama included:

   . . . The Lone Ranger

   . . . Sergeant Preston of the Yukon

   . . . The Green Hornet (a forerunner of today's superheroes)

   . . . Little Orphan Annie

   . . . Jack Armstrong, All-American Boy

   . . . Boston Blackie (a hard-boiled detective)

At your local library you can find recordings of these and many other shows. As a first step in doing radio drama, get some of those records and listen carefully to them to learn about radio techniques. Then make up some radio adventures of your own. Consider such characters as:

   . . . The Lone Astronaut (an outer space troubleshooter)

   . . . Sergeant Bilsky of 42nd Street (a modern policeman working in the city)

   . . . The _____ name any color _____ _____ name any animal or insect _____ (a superhero/ine).

   . . . Ms. Annie (a modern-day little girl who isn't frightened of anything)

   . . . Jane Armstrong, All-American Girl

   . . . Philadelphia Flakie (a bumbling detective who is a soft touch.)

Serials. An excellent way to get started in radio drama is to do your program—usually an adventure story—as a series consisting of a number of short episodes. Usually an installment begins with the hero or heroine in some sort of deep difficulty and ends with a new problem or pending disaster. Thus a serial leaves your audience "hanging," wondering what will happen next. "To find out, tune in tomorrow." Many card and gift shops sell "letter tapes" and "letter cassettes," which are simply *short* tapes with a five- or ten-minute recording time. You might want to consider taping your serial on some of these and even sending them to a friend or relatives in another city.

Docu-Dramas. Read up on an important historical event, then, through radio, recreate the scene to bring the listener directly there. Some events which you might dramatize include:

... the Boston Tea Party.
... Paul Revere's ride.
... General Lee surrenders to General Grant to end the Civil War.
... your own birth. (Interview your parents to get information on that one.)

Scenes From the Newspaper. Read today's paper and look for a story that seems to have a lot of drama in it, either a front-page story or something from the sports section. Then turn it into a radio play. In another variation of the radio play, you can do a make-believe newscast presenting the news, with interviews and comments woven in.

Other Ideas for Radio Plays.

- Deadly gas has gotten loose in the factory.
- The mayor has been stealing funds from the city.
- Army life.
- Life inside the human bloodstream.
- Grass attacks a lawn mower.
- Somebody is kidnapped.
- Something is stolen.
- People start acting in a *very* peculiar way.

Writing the Script. Radio theater can be done as **improvisation,** with actors and actresses making up lines as they go along, but we don't recommend it. Often improvised radio plays get kind of sloppy, or awkward pauses develop when people can't think of things to say. While such problems may seem natural in a stage play, they sound very bad on radio. It's better, we believe, to go to the trouble of writing out a script for your show.

Most of the scriptwriting techniques described in Chapter 4 will work for radio, so review that chapter briefly before beginning work. In addition to the characters in your play, you will want to add lines for the *narrator* if you use one. Also put into your script the *sound effects* you want to use. At the scriptwriting stage, don't worry about how you will achieve the sound effects or whether or not they seem practical. If your plan calls for the sound of an atomic bomb going off in the next room, write it in:

SOUND EFFECT: Huge explosion.

If you want to use background music, write in a description of the mood you want to create.

MUSIC: Romantic, violins playing.

You can always look for a specific piece of music to fit that mood, but sometimes you can describe the particular piece you want from the start.

MUSIC: "The Marines' Hymn" sung by a choir.

Above all, remember to *write visually*. Put in all the visual details you think you will need, and then add a few more to make your radio play vivid. It's a good idea to have somebody read your first draft of the script and make suggestions, or assemble a cast and have them read through your draft and make suggestions. When you have the script polished the way you want it, try to get copies run off for everybody in your cast and crew.

Producing Your Radio Play. Once the script is done you can start the process of turning it into an actual drama—producing it. In addition to the usual cast, you will also need several other people, including a *technician* (somebody who runs your tape recorder), one or more *sound-effects people*, and a *music director* to supply music on cue. Somebody—probably you—also needs to be the director who supervises the whole operation.

Equipment. It's relatively easy to do a radio play on an ordinary cassette tape recorder, which you may already have around home. If you don't own one, you may be able to borrow one from a friend or school. When you have the tape recorder, experiment with it and with the microphone to learn how to get good recordings. If you get too close to the mike, the sound will blast and become blurry. If you get too far from it, voices sound like they're coming from inside a phone booth. Unless you have a fancy tape recorder with several microphones, you'll need to arrange your recording studio (probably the dining-room table) so everybody can get close to it. Again, practice several scenes until you are happy with the results.

Sound Effects. These can be created three ways:

1. From records. Your local library probably has sound-effects records you can borrow, records with everything from a marching band to a Ping-Pong game on them. You may find some of the sound effects you need already recorded.

2. For real. If you can borrow a second tape recorder, go out into the world and make actual recordings of the sounds you need. For example, if your script calls for the sound of a bulldozer plowing away, go find one and record it. (Hint: Record your sound effects in the actual order you will use them in the play. That will make life simpler when you are recording the drama itself.)

3. In the studio. In the old days of radio, sound-effects people developed all sorts of ways of creating the sounds they needed. Thunder could be recreated by shaking a piece of tin near the microphone. Hoofbeats were usually done by someone pounding coconut shells on his chest. Some studios had little model doors which could be slammed close to the mike for that sound. Footsteps were created by tapping with a wooden pencil on a wood block or tabletop. If your sound person enjoys it, have him or her create as many studio sounds as possible.

Music. Search for recordings that create the mood you want and stack them up in the order you will need them. The records can be played at the appropriate points in the play. (Place the speaker of your record player close enough to the microphone that the sound will be clear.) Again, if you have an extra tape recorder, you may want to record the music on tape, in the order it will be played, perhaps even alternating with the sound effects, all in advance. Then when you are actually recording the play on tape recorder #1, all you have to do is punch the buttons on recorder #2 to create the sound effects and music you want.

Recording the Play. Prepare carefully and rehearse carefully and everything should go well. As director, you may want to develop a set of hand signals to use with your cast and crew: point to people when they are to speak; signal them to talk louder or softer; point to the sound person when an effect is needed; signal the music director to raise or lower the volume. If people make a mistake, don't worry about it, just back up the tape a bit and do the scene over again until you get it right.

"Broadcasting" Your Radio Play. The most interesting kind of "broadcast" for your play will simply be to play the tape back—for the actors, for parents, for friends, for your class at school. But you might want to look for a wider audience. Many schools, for instance, have an intercom or loudspeaker system that lets the principal make announcements in all the rooms at once. If your play is good enough, you might convince him or her to play your tape "on the air" for the whole school. You might even make an appointment to play your tape for the manager of a local radio station. All stations must give over a certain amount of time to "community service" broadcasts. Perhaps the manager will agree that your neighborhood radio play is a community service and deserves to be presented as an actual radio broadcast.

Video Drama

When television first came on the scene over thirty years ago, it was strictly a studio business, done with bulky cameras at the TV station. In the past two decades, however, lightweight, portable video cameras and video tape recorders have been developed that have brought television-making out into the street. Equally important, the invention of video tape recording has made it possible for broadcasters to collect, edit, and save scenes for showing at a later time. The biggest breakthrough of all has come in the development of home video recorders and cameras, so that it is possible to have a TV studio right in your living room.

Home video equipment is still quite expensive, and not everybody has access to it. Yet, we'll guess that if you are interested in developing neighborhood television, you probably can get access to equipment in one of three places:

1) home video equipment, either your own or that owned by the parents of your friends.
2) portable video equipment used by your school.
3) equipment available at a local cable television outlet.

The last one—#3—requires more discussion. Cable television—sometimes called subscription TV—has reached most parts of the country and puts a great many new channels on an ordinary television set. By federal law, cable TV companies must also provide some channels for local use, so if you have cable TV in your area, you'll see some channels that are run by schools, towns and cities, and by the cable company itself. You'll also find that the cable company has its own broadcast studio and will record your play for you—free—and play it over one of its public channels for thousands of viewers. (The cable companies also offer courses in how to produce your own TV program, and if you're really interested in learning about television—maybe even thinking about it as a career—we suggest that you sign up for one.)

In any case, if you are excited about doing a television drama, look around. We think you'll locate equipment pretty quickly once you start your search.

Ideas for Television Plays.

Your Own Drama. The best starting point for television plays are dramas that you have written and produced yourself. Perhaps you have written a full scripted play as suggested in the previous chapter, or you and your friends have put together a collection of short plays. Further, you have produced them—having actors and actresses learn lines, get into costumes, use makeup, and so on—so your play has been on stage, seen by dozens or hundreds of people. Now, why not make it more permanent by putting it on video? To adapt your play for television, you simply have to think about how you want it to appear and jot down ideas and instructions for your camera and sound crews (see next section). Then present your play for the camera, just as if the camera were a real audience.

Commercials. Television ads are a lot of fun to do, and you can probably think of a dozen different ads you'd like to videotape. Make a list of the ten most ridiculous ads on television: What about the one where the little man rows his boat around in a toilet? Or the one where a housewife is embarrassed by "ring around the collar"? Or those soda and beer taste tests where folks decide they like the sponsor's product better? Or the automobile ad where it looks as if you get a panther and a sexy lady free with your new car? Write a series of scripts satirizing—poking fun at—these ads.

Or,

Write some real commercials and ads for things you want to promote or sell. You might make a commercial for one of your own plays, inviting people to attend. Or you could tape an appeal for students at your school to buy the yearbook or participate in a car wash. (The tapes might be shown in a public place like the school lobby.) Or you might talk to the public librarian and make some taped commercials for Book Week or for a summer reading program.

Satires of Television Programs. One stage beyond poking fun at TV commercials is doing a spoof on a whole show. Make another list of ten: the ten most ridiculous shows on television. List shows that are supposed to be funny, but aren't; shows where people make fools of themselves; shows that are too filled with violence or mushy love. Then make up your own shows that make fun of the silly characteristics of these.

News Programs. These aren't exactly "plays," but in our neighborhood, the cable television carries several news shows written by junior and senior high school students. One of these is a satirical show, making fun of the news much like television's *Saturday Night* show. The other program is straight: the news of the week reviewed by young people. In both cases, though these are not "plays," they involve careful planning and the writing of a script.

Documentaries and Historical Recreations. As we suggested with radio drama, you can also use television to bring history to life. Consider doing an *author interview,* in which an author you enjoy reading or would like to know more about appears on television and is quizzed by some of his or her fans. Or choose an event in history—preferably something that happened indoors, not a grand-scale battle—and do a "you are there" broadcast about it.

Talk Shows and Panels. Again, these are not "plays" in a strict sense, but they involve a good deal of careful planning and some roleplaying and acting. For example, you might adapt the author interview to a *talk show* format, and have the writer talk about his or her work. Or choose a topic of current interest—say, *Energy and the Environment*— and set up a talk show with make-believe experts giving their opinions. If your teacher will allow it, do your next report as a video taped *panel discussion* between yourself and some of your friends.

Puppet Shows. As you know from real television, puppet shows are very attractive on TV. Consider writing a play for television using puppets as the actors and actresses. You'll find that puppetry is easy to do on TV and it cuts down on the complications of scenes, sets, props, and even actors and actresses.

Other Shows. Borrow the videotape equipment and record other shows that you and your friends do: magic shows, the neighborhood carnival, writers reading their own work, reader's theater enactments of short stories and plays.

Planning and Scriptwriting. Scriptwriting for television is quite similar to writing any play script. So before you begin, review the ideas suggested in Chapter 4. However, you'll need to add instructions for your camera operator as well. You can do this by simply writing in the kind of picture or "video" you want:

Video: Closeup on Rebecca's face.

The kinds of shots you can get will depend very much on the complexity of the video equipment you are using. The very simplest outfits will simply let you set up the camera and "film" the play from a single point of view. If you are working in a cable TV studio, you may have several different cameras, some with zoom lenses, and a switching device to flip back and forth from one picture to another. Since we don't know what kind of equipment you'll be using, we'll leave it to you to ask somebody who knows what kinds of video effects you can get.

Our basic recommendation in writing your script: *Don't get too fancy with the video.* While it might be tempting to build in all sorts of interesting close-ups and zoom shots or to have many changes of scene in your play, resist the temptation. Don't try to imitate some of the slick programs you see on commercial television. We recommend that for your first drama you stick to a one-scene play, all of which takes place in a single room. After you've had success with that, consider getting more elaborate.

Production. When the script is done, get copies run off for your actors and actresses, plus the video crew. You'll need one or more camera people, at least one person to handle sound, a **director**—probably you—and, in all likelihood, some adults who know how to use the video equipment.

When you tape, *present your drama in small chunks.* Don't try to get a twenty-minute play on tape without stopping. Rather, shoot the play in segments that are two or three minutes long at the most. For each scene or segment, we suggest the following procedure:

1) *Walk-through.* This is a slow acting out of the scene, with pauses every few seconds to make certain your camera and sound people know what they are getting. The sound person will want to check the voice level to make certain the microphone is close enough to the actors. The camera person can peer through the camera to see what the scene will look like on the tube. When everybody is set, then make your:

2) *Practice tape.* Roll the video recorder and do the scene all the way through, stopping only if something goes completely wrong. Mistakes are OK here; you can learn from them. When the taping is done, rewind the video recorder and watch the scene. Evaluate what you have done. Was the sound good? What about the camera angles? Did the actors and actresses do their parts correctly? If everything went perfectly (and as you get experienced, it often will), then you can consider the practice scene a "take" and go on to the next scene. More often than not, however, you'll need to make a:

3) *Final tape.* This one's for real, folks. No more giggling in the background over mistakes. No more saying "oops" aloud when somebody forgets his or her lines. Get all your cast and crew to concentrate hard on the job so it goes well. Of course, if you botch this time, you can always erase and retape (something you can't do if you're making a movie as discussed in the next section). But try to make #3 your final take. Otherwise, the whole procedure of videotaping may become quite boring.

How long will it take? If you follow this three-step procedure, you may spend two or three hours making a twenty minute tape. You can do it quicker, but the quality won't be as good.

Finally, when it's all done, you'll want to show the tape. The audience for your program will depend on the equipment you use, but you may consider the following range:

- home video, playing the show back through your (or somebody else's) family television.

- closed-circuit television around your school.
- setting up the equipment in a public place like a school lobby, the library corridor, or a bank lobby, then showing it to passersby.
- as an exhibit in a talent fair.
- over a local cable television channel.

Moviemaking

Making a movie. Ah, yes. Fond memories—not so fond, really—of Uncle Fud unpacking his projector to show vacation films. Aunt Minnie and the kids waving at the camera with the Grand Canyon out of focus in the background. Delays when the film breaks and Uncle Fud tries to patch it with Scotch tape. "Just one more reel," he says, after you've already sat through five boring reels for over an hour.

Well, home movies *can* be a bore, but the problem is often with the imagination of the filmmaker rather than something having to do with the camera or the idea of making a movie. "Home" movie equipment—usually a camera and projector using super 8 millimeter film—has become technically quite sophisticated over the years while remaining easy to use. For example, most movie cameras now have built-in "electric eyes" which monitor the amount of light coming in and take care of setting the lens opening for you. There is even an "instant movie" camera, which develops the film right away so you can view your movie minutes after you have made it. And filmmaking remains relatively inexpensive: You can make a good "one reeler" (a three-minute film) for a little over ten dollars.

In making a movie, you don't want to imitate Uncle Fud and fill the screen with a bunch of vacation pictures loosely held together. At the same time, it's not a good idea to imitate what you see at your local movie theater either, because commercial films are done with very complicated equipment and shot over a period of months—even years. If you try to do a full-scale film like "Star Wars" or "Superman," you'll probably just be disappointed with the results.

What you *can* do with super 8 millimeter equipment is make some short, lively, visually interesting films that will be very entertaining to an audience.

For example, here are some ideas that will work well for short movies done with "home" equipment:

Silent Films. It's tough to do a "talkie" with super 8 millimeter equipment. Though a few cameras are equipped with a microphone and can record sound as well as images, most can't, and it's difficult to get good quality sound anyway. We recommend that you do an old-time silent movie, though one that can be made modern through the choice of story. In doing this sort of film, your actors and actresses will have to be skilled at **pantomime.** (See Chapter 1.) They will mime actions and reactions so the audience can tell what is going on. (You may also want to add *titles* or *subtitles*, just like old-time movies. To do this, simply write the dialogue on a piece of posterboard or even a chalkboard and film it for two or three seconds. Silent films can include:

Melodrama. (See Chapter 2) High-action adventure tales with villains and villainesses, heroes and heroines and the forces of good and evil fighting for supremacy.

Creature Feature. A silent movie about a horrible monster (one of your friends in ghoulish makeup) that threatens the world.

Slapstick. Wild and wacky humor with lots of chases, make-believe fights, and even pies in the face or shaving-cream fights.

Modern Adventures. Detective shows or outer space dramas done in pantomime.

Moods and Impressions. Film is a good way to catch a number of images and put them close together. Study some TV commercials for examples of this. For instance, for a number of years Pepsi-Cola has shown advertisements consisting of a number of very short shots of people having a good time while drinking Pepsi. The whole idea is to create an image of the "Pepsi generation" as fun-loving, good-time guys and gals. Without being as corny as a Pepsi ad, consider ways in which you can create a mood or impression on film. For example, you might take a favorite poem, read it into a tape recorder, then make a film with images to match the mood of the poem. Or make a film with images to match the lyrics of one of your favorite songs, then show the film and play the record at the same time.

Character Sketch. Follow a friend around with a camera for a day, shooting him or her in various aspects of life. When you have completed a reel of film about this friend, write a character sketch describing what the person is like, what he or she means to you. Then show the film and read your character sketch at the same time. Or, do a:

Place Sketch. Make a film about an unusual or interesting place: an auto race track, the beach, school, your neighborhood. With the camera, catch images that seem to you to represent the spirit or mood of the place. When you have completed the film, write a script to go along with it, your "character sketch" of a place rather than a person.

Novelty Films. We can't, in this book, describe all the novel and unusual things you can do with a movie camera. If you're interested, go to the library and get a book on filmmaking that will tell you in detail how to do such unusual films as:

Disappearing Act Films. In these you stop the camera from time to time, hold it steady, and have people or objects removed from the scene before you resume filming. The result on the screen shows people and things vanishing into thin air. (Reverse the process and they materialize out of nothingness—a great technique for outer-space films.)

Time Lapse. With the camera mounted on a tripod, you take just a few frames of film at intervals throughout the day. The result is that action is apparently speeded up.

Slow Motion Films. These films actually take more pictures in a shorter period of time so that things seem to happen more slowly than usual. Consider using slow motion to show surprise in grim detail as your villain realizes his plan has failed.

Cartoons. With the right kind of camera (check a library book or the instruction manual with your camera) you can do your own animated cartoons, drawing many sketches, each one showing a bit of motion, then photographing them one at a time. Animation requires a great deal of time and patience, but if you have both of those, you can make an exciting short film.

Object Animation. Using a technique similar to shooting a cartoon, you can make objects move: tables and chairs dance; coffee cups become filled with no person present; typewriters send messages on their own.

Planning and Filming. The big DON'T: Don't simply borrow a movie camera, load it with film, and head off into the sunrise to make a film. Moviemaking requires a great deal of careful advance planning, and you need to think out—scene by scene—what you want to have happen. You can write out a script for your film if you want, but another technique that many young filmmakers find useful is to do something called a "storyboard" (Figure 4). This is simply a sketched version of what you want the movie to be like, scene by scene. You can use stick figures if you want to, but you should try to show whether you want the camera to take a *full-length shot* (one that shows your players from head to toe), a *close-up*, or something in between. You can also show the *camera angle* (perhaps you want one scene shot from up in a tree or from a rooftop). On your storyboard, also indicate how long you think the scene will take. We recommend that you keep most of your scenes quite short, perhaps as short as ten seconds. Keeping the scenes short cuts down on the possibilities of making a mistake, and also helps to make your film interesting and lively.

Writing the storyboard may take you some time; you may spend a week or more doing it. Making the film itself will also take time. Just as it is with making a videotape, you should plan on spending several hours just to make something that will last two or three minutes on the screen.

Before you film, it is important to become familiar with the movie camera that you have begged or borrowed. Read the instruction booklet carefully and make certain you know how to work the various buttons. If you can, borrow a tripod—a three-legged stand—and mount the camera on that for steadiness. If your budget will permit it, shoot a practice roll of

FIGURE 4

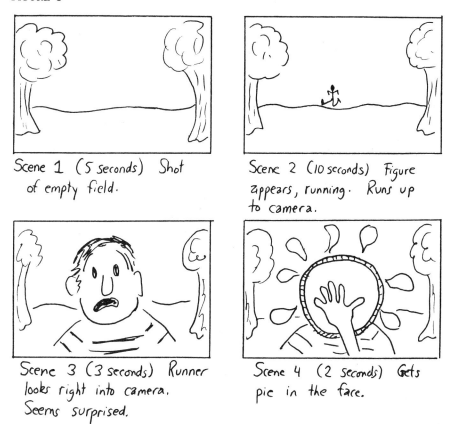

Scene 1 (5 seconds) Shot of empty field.

Scene 2 (10 seconds) Figure appears, running. Runs up to camera.

Scene 3 (3 seconds) Runner looks right into camera. Seems surprised.

Scene 4 (2 seconds) Gets pie in the face.

film to get the feel of the camera. Make close-ups and long-distance shots. Take film of people, objects, and animals. Practice *panning* (swinging the camera from side to side) slowly and then rapidly. If the camera has a *zoom* lens, experiment with that and see what effects you can get. Then, when the film comes back from the developer, view it and evaluate your mistakes carefully.

When you are finally ready to make a film, round up your cast and get them into costumes, if any. In addition to the actors and actresses, you'll also need a person to operate the camera and a director (though you can be both camera person and director if you want). Then shoot the film, scene by scene, following your storyboard. We suggest that you rehearse each scene and film it in three stages:

1) *Slow-motion walk-through.* In this one, the actors and actresses move very slowly while the camera person peers through the viewfinder to see what the scene will look like. Does everything fit? Are any motions cut out of the scene? You may want to readjust your camera angles after this.

2) *Dress rehearsal.* Now do the scene up to speed, again with the camera person following the action. Make certain everything is done correctly, since this is the last chance to make changes.

3) *Film.* Call "Ready on the set!" to get everybody quiet and concentrating. Then, "Action!" At that point, the actors act, the camera rolls, and you get a "take."

Of course, not every "take" will be perfect. Sometimes things will go awry: The cameraman had his thumb over the lens; the lead actress's wig fell off. In that case, you'll need to do the scene again, and when the film comes back from the developer, you'll need to *edit.* To do this, you'll need to borrow a film editor, which is simply a device that lets you cut the film to eliminate the parts you don't want and then paste the film back together. We won't go into the details here; simply read the instructions that come with the editor.

Once the film has been edited, you're almost ready for a showing. You may want to tape-record some background music to go along with the movie, or if you have written a script, practice reading it while the film shows to make certain the film and script last the same length of time. Then round up a crowd from your neighborhood and have movie night. We can just about guarantee that if you've followed the steps we've outlined here and planned your film carefully, your audience will be much more appreciative than they are for Uncle Fud's home movies. They may even call for "more!"

Part II

Getting the Show on the Road

How to Put on a Play

So you've written a play! Perhaps you have prepared a script for a full-length play of several acts. Or you and your friends have each written scripts for a series of one-act plays. Or you've made puppets and worked out plans for an improvised puppet show. Or you've done any of the dozens of playmaking projects we have suggested in Part I of this book. Now it's time to go from planning to production, from thinking about the play itself to considering how to present your play to an audience (and how to make certain you'll actually have an audience to watch your presentation). Some people think that all the fun and creativity ends with play*making*, that the *putting on* part is just boring and a lot of hard work. It *is* hard work, but it needn't be boring or uninteresting. In fact, you can be just as creative in staging your play as you were in writing it, and nothing is more satisfying to a writer than seeing something he or she designed on paper spring to life through an excellent stage production. Now read on and consider ways and means of translating your ideas into a show that will be entertaining to your audience and satisfying to you, the writer.

The Backstage "Drama." As a play proceeds on stage, there is also a kind of drama going on behind the scenes, a play with its own cast of characters. In the theater, the backstage cast may include such people as the **stage manager,** who is in charge of the lights, sound effects, raising and lowering the curtain, and so on; the **prompter,** who reads the script silently and helps actors and actresses who forget their lines; the **property master** or **mistress,** who makes certain all the furniture and gadgets needed in the play are in the right place at the right time; the **wardrobe mistress** or **master,** who keeps the costumes in order and ready for changes; **stage hands,** who supply the muscle to change scenes while the curtains are closed; even a **call boy** or **girl** who lets actors and actresses know just before it is time for them to go on stage.

It may be that in your neighborhood theater production you will want to have all these people to help you out. But most of the time, a smaller crew will be quite adequate and less complicated to work with. We suggest that you divide all the jobs into two categories and assign them to one or the other of two backstage characters, the **producer** and the **director,** with one taking care of all the arrangements for putting on the play and the other being responsible for working with the actors and actresses. If you are the author of a play, you'll probably want to take on the director's role, since that will let you control what's called the "artistic quality" of the show by making certain the play that appears on stage is the same one you wrote. However, if you are good at organizing things, or if you like to build things and make things with your hands, you might prefer to be the producer, handling arrangements. Or, you might choose both to produce and to direct your show, handling all the responsibilities yourself. No matter how you arrange it, you will find it useful to divide all the jobs associated with putting on your play into two basic categories: the *producer's jobs* and the *director's jobs*. We'll discuss each of these in detail in the next two sections.

The Producer. If you were the producer of a New York Broadway production, your first job would be to go out and raise several million dollars to fund the production. If you were a Hollywood film producer, you might have to come up with as much as twenty or thirty million bucks. In fact, in real theater and film, the producer is often just the money man or woman, the person who finds the dollars necessary to get the show rolling. The chances are, however, that you will do your neighborhood theater production on a shoestring budget, spending very little money at all, and your producer can turn his or her attention to other matters.

The producer will need to handle such matters as: running off copies of the script (if you are using scripts), building or supervising the construction of scenery and lighting, finding and/or making a stage, getting out publicity, finding chairs for the audience to sit on, printing up and selling tickets (if you're charging money for admission). We have given you a checklist of the producer's responsibilities in Figure 5. Not everything listed will apply to every production, so the director and producer should study the

FIGURE 5

The Producer's Checklist

( ) Run off copies of the script for each actor/actress.
( ) Find a place to stage the play or create a stage.
( ) Build scenery (with help from others).
( ) Locate any needed props for the play.
( ) Find costumes if needed.
( ) Arrange for actors' and actresses' makeup if needed.
( ) Prepare advertising for the play.
( ) Prepare tickets.
( ) Recruit ushers if needed.
( ) Arrange for printing of programs if needed.
( ) Get refreshments and somebody to sell them.
( ) Assist the director at rehearsals and during the show.
( ) Serve as a prompter if needed during the show.
( ) (add other responsibilities you think of)
( ) _____
( ) _____

Getting the Show on the Road   *115*

checklist and make one of their own so that from the very beginning the producer knows what his or her responsibilities will be. Some "how to" ideas for producers will also be found elsewhere in this section. (See *The Elements of Stagecraft*, *Advertising Your Play*, and *Curtain Up!*)

The Director. The director, as his/her title suggests, *directs* the actors and actresses, helping the script written on the page become a living, breathing play. In neighborhood theater, the director has to be especially careful not to turn into a bossy type, thinking he or she can order people around or getting angry if they don't do exactly what is wanted. As a director, you should see yourself as helping people make the most of their talents, coaching and guiding them, not pushing and shoving. The director's responsibilities come in three stages:

1. *Casting.* This simply means choosing the people who will take various roles in your play, and it is a very important step. You want to make certain that you get the right people for the right parts and that your actors and actresses can handle the roles assigned to them. In true theater, the director will often have **auditions,** in which people try out for parts and the people who seem best are selected. More often, with neighborhood theater, you'll be faced with the problem of recruiting enough people to fill all the parts. (Sometimes, in fact, you may have one person playing several different parts, and you, the director, may need to take on a small or large part yourself.) You can find actors and actresses simply by talking about your play with your friends in the neighborhood and at school. Depending on how many people you need, you might even ask a teacher to announce your plans and ask for volunteers to participate.

There are no set rules for casting your play. Just use common sense to guide you in getting people matched up with the right parts. Even if you don't hold auditions, you might want to ask people to read a portion of your script aloud, just to see how it sounds. Do people read in a loud clear voice that can be heard at the back of a room, or in a quiet, timid voice? Give big parts to the people with loud voices and smaller parts to the quiet ones. Do people read with lots of expression or do they simply read in a plain, flat voice? Again, give the big parts to the people who can read with some dramatic flair. Assign taller people to adult roles; shorter ones should play the kids. Sometimes it's good simply to assemble all the actors and actresses, tell them what the parts are, and let them express a preference. As director, though, you reserve the right to make final decisions about casting. (If you happen to have more volunteers than you have parts, you might want to appoint one or two people as **understudies,** who attend most of the rehearsals and are prepared to step in and take a role if somebody drops out of the play.)

2. *Rehearsing.* Chances are, your actors and actresses will want to get the rehearsals over with quickly so they can get on with the show. *Don't let them rush you.* Rehearsing is a *must* part of putting on a play, and if you skimp on this part, you may be sorry later because of a poor performance.

Your first rehearsal should simply be a **reader's theater** enactment of the script, with your cast seated about the room reading their parts in turn. As the play progresses, tell people how you would like lines read—loud or soft? happy or sad?—and encourage them to put expression into their reading. But in the early stages, don't interrupt too often, or the rehearsal will get boring.

For the second rehearsal, try a **walk-through,** with people holding scripts and reading from them, but moving about as if they were actually on a stage. For this rehearsal, work closely with your producer and block out your rehearsal area—maybe your living room—as if it were an actual stage. It might be useful to use theater terms to talk about the actual parts of the stage—**upstage, downstage, center stage,** and so on (see Figure 6). If your director is a hustler, he or she may already have some scenery and props ready for your actors and actresses to use, but probably that will have to wait until later.

The number of additional rehearsals required will depend in large measure on how long and complicated your play is. If it's a short play, your cast may be able to memorize its lines quickly so you can move directly to

FIGURE 6

Stage Terms

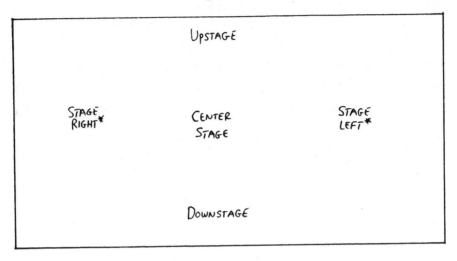

°NOTE: The left and right sides of the stage are described from the point of view of the actors and actresses as they face the audience. The director needs to remember that, especially if he or she is standing where the audience is supposed to be.

a **dress rehearsal,** where you dress in costumes, practice putting on makeup, and present your play exactly as you would to an audience. More likely, however, you will need several rehearsals before you hold your final dress rehearsal. At these sessions, plan carefully what you want to do. Gradually get people to stop using their scripts and to do their lines from memory. Show them the kinds of gestures you want them to use in their acting. You might even want to begin rehearsals with some dramatic warm-ups (see Chapter 1) to get people into the mood of their part. You'll probably also need to keep the rehearsals reasonably short and moving along at a good pace so people don't get bored. Also, as important as rehearsals are, you can over-rehearse your cast, striving for so much perfection that the cast gets sick of the show (and sick of you, too). So use your judgment, and when you think the show is *almost* good enough for an audience, hold the dress rehearsal, in which you go through the play from beginning to end, with no interruptions, just as you would before a live audience.

3. *The Presentation.* Most of the director's work is done by the time the curtain goes up and the play is presented to an actual audience. If you have rehearsed well, if your actors and actresses have learned their parts, if your producer has done his or her part, the show will go well and you, the director, can simply watch it from backstage. But you also need to be alert to problems. If your lead actor or actress gets jitters or stage fright, assure him or her that everything will be all right. If somebody forgets lines in the middle of a crucial scene, prompt from the side until things are rolling again. There's an old saying in the theater, "If something can go wrong, it will," so be prepared to step in and take whatever action is necessary to solve on-the-spot problems.

And . . . remember that the show will probably never go quite as well as you wanted it to. Don't be disappointed or angry if you get a less-than-perfect performance. Remember that this is neighborhood theater, not a Broadway performance.

The Elements of Stagecraft

Stagecraft—the mechanics of getting a play on stage, complete with sets, props, costumes, and makeup—is the principal responsibility of the producer in a neighborhood theater production, but the director should work very closely with the producer to make certain that all these theatrical "trappings" fit with the play so the presentation will look good as well as be acted successfully.

The Stage. Five hundred years ago in England, roving theater companies put on religious plays using nothing more than the back of their horse-drawn wagons as a stage. When the performance was over, they simply stuffed all their props into the wagon and left, moving on to the next village.

Since that time, theater stages have become much more complex. If you've seen a play produced by a professional theater company or by a serious amateur group, you probably know how complicated a stage can be, with several curtains, walls and scenery that drop down from above, multicolored lighting, and in some cases, even revolving platforms for scene changes.

The simple puppet stage shown in Figure 7 shows the basic elements of the stage as it has developed in modern times. At the front of the stage is something called the **proscenium arch,** which creates a window effect and frames the stage. Immediately behind it is the main curtain which rises and falls at the beginnings of the acts and scenes. The back of the stage may be another curtain or it can be flat or a wall on which some background scenery has been painted. If you enjoy puppetry, you might want to build a rather elaborate stage, complete with special lighting effects done with Christmas-tree bulbs.

For most neighborhood theater presentations, the stage does not need to be anything near that fancy; in fact, the less complicated your stage, the better. For some productions, you may not need a "stage" at all. You can simply identify a piece of ground or a part of a room as the area where your play will take place and imagine the setting. You might even want to seat your audience in a circle around that place and conduct what is called "theater in the round" and the actors and actresses do not have to worry about moving "upstage" and "downstage" or avoiding turning their backs to the audience, which sits on all sides. But if you want to be a bit more formal, you can clear one end of a room of furniture (except your stage furniture) and face the chairs of the audience toward it. Outdoors, consider laying out a garden hose or a piece of rope to mark the boundaries of this make-believe stage.

In the true theater, many actors and actresses prefer that sort of "bare bones" stage or imaginary stage, because it forces the audience to concen-

A Basic Puppet Stage

MAKE STAGE FROM CARDBOARD BOX

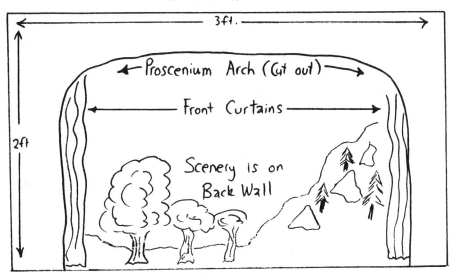

Proscenium Arch (Cut out)

Front Curtains

Scenery is on Back Wall

2ft

3ft.

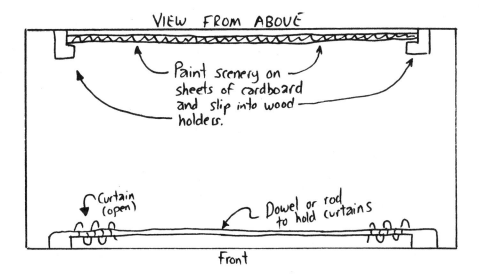

VIEW FROM ABOVE

Paint scenery on sheets of cardboard and slip into wood holders.

Curtain (open)

Dowel or rod to hold curtains

Front

FIGURE 7

FIGURE 8

trate on them and to become involved in the play by visualizing the scene.
For those simple stages, you may want to make some cards to tell the
audience what to imagine. These can be propped on an art easel if you
have one (Figure 8).

But you may want to have something a little more formal as a stage,
something to give you and the actors and actresses a feeling that there is a
place where all the action is happening. You may also want to have painted
scenery and backdrops to give your audience a better idea of the location
of the play. If you are giving your play out-of-doors, you might be able to
erect a simple canopy or tarpaulin (a "tarp") to serve as a stage. (A neighbor
who goes camping may have one you can borrow.) The background can be
painted on an old sheet and hung at the back of the canopy (Figure 9).

FIGURE 9

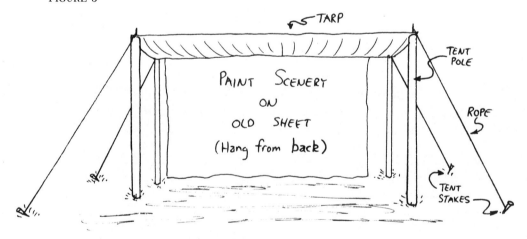

Another kind of stage for indoor or outdoor use can be made from large sheets of cardboard. Visit an appliance or department store and ask for some discarded packing cartons—the bigger the better. Cut off the ends of the cartons, then slice down one edge to open the box into a large sheet (Figure 10). Tack strips of scrap wood (sometimes called "furring" by carpenters) onto the back of the cardboard to strengthen it; then prop it up with a stick or pole. You can paint this **flat** (as it is called in the theater)

FIGURE 10

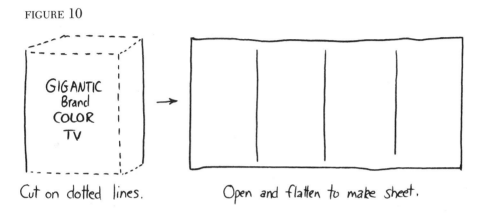

Cut on dotted lines.   Open and flatten to make sheet.

either a plain color or with a background scene (Figure 11). If you have a very large box to begin with (such as the kind a refrigerator comes in), you can form the panels of the box into a semicircle to create your stage (Figure 12). You might also consider making your flats as cutout shapes to represent trees, objects, even buildings, and scattering them about the stage to create a kind of three-dimensional background (Figure 13).

A word on painting your scenery and backgrounds: first, if you don't like to draw or paint yourself, get some help from an artistic friend who would like to tackle this job, which involves painting on a large scale. However, remember that your background merely needs to create the impression of a scene; this doesn't have to be a masterpiece of color and detail as if it were going to hang in an art museum. Often a few strokes of green and brown may be enough to represent trees, and some blue (dark blue, not

FIGURE 11

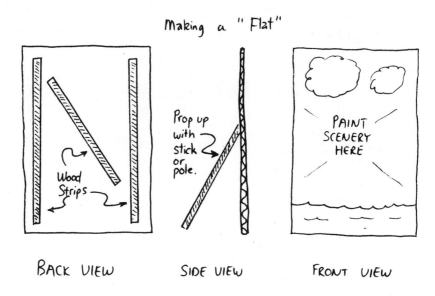

Making a " Flat "

BACK VIEW   SIDE VIEW   FRONT VIEW

FIGURE 12

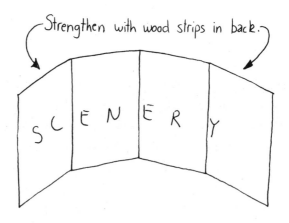

Strengthen with wood strips in back.

Putting on a Play

FIGURE 13

robin's egg) may be enough to indicate a lake or a river or the sea. When you or your artist are painting on large sheets of cloth or cardboard, you may tend to draw too small and in too much detail. As you paint, back off twenty or thirty meters from time to time to get the overall impression of your work.

For painting cardboard, poster paints work well. You can probably get a supply of the powder (you have to mix the paints with water yourself) from an art teacher at school, or you can buy the paints ready-mixed at the art- or school-supply store. A good bet for painting either cloth or cardboard is ordinary Latex (or "water-based") house paint, either indoor or outdoor paint. If you ask the members of your cast to look around home, they can probably locate half-used cans of paint in a rainbow of colors, leftovers from house or apartment decorating. But also remember what they taught you in art class: if you have the three primary colors—red, yellow, and blue—plus some white, you can mix just about any shade and tint of paint.

Lighting is also an important part of stagecraft. In the professional theater, lighting is used skillfully to create a very bright scene that focuses the

Getting the Show on the Road   **125**

attention of the audience, seated in the dark. Through the use of light filters and dimmers, a professional lighting expert can create the illusion of sunrise, sunset, or even moonglow. For neighborhood theater, such effects can also be simulated if you have the right equipment. However, do not fool around with lighting and electricity without the supervision of an adult who knows a good deal about electricity. Electrical equipment is very dangerous and there is no margin for error.

For basic lighting, you might want a simple spotlight trained on the stage. If you're working out-of-doors, you may find that there is already a floodlight mounted on the corner of the house that can be turned to shine on your stage. Another good bet is a portable floodlight (Figure 14) which many people have on hand to light up their houses during the Christmas/

FIGURE 14

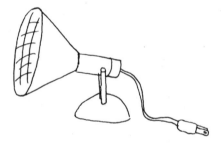

Chanukah holiday season. If you can get several of these lights, one can be used to illuminate the stage from in front, while others can be placed at the sides and foot of the stage to serve as footlights (Figure 15). Different colored bulbs are available for these floodlights, so you can create a variety of color effects. Alternatively, you can find pieces of colored, transparent paper or plastic to place over a white floodlight to create color filters. Another good source of colored lights is Christmas-tree bulbs. (A few blue lights hung offstage, for instance, will do a beautiful job creating the effect of a moonlit night.) Finally, if you want to create some lights especially for

FIGURE 15

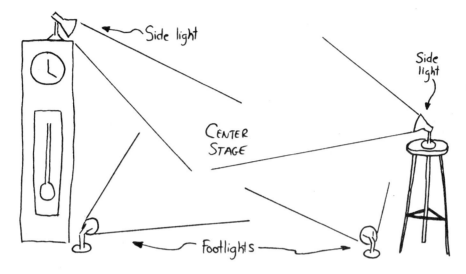

Side light

Side light

CENTER STAGE

Footlights

your neighborhood theater group, you can make light fixtures out of a large (#10) tin can and an ordinary lightbulb socket purchased at a hardware store (Figure 16). Once again, don't undertake an electrical project without an adult who really knows what he or she is doing.

With the scenery and lighting set, you may want to think about having a curtain for your stage, something that can hide the set from the audience and signal when the play begins and when the acts end. The simplest kind of curtain is called the Kid-Sister-and-Brother-Curtain, and it consists of having two younger kids hold a bedsheet in front of your stage (Figure 17).

However, the younger ones are not always helpful and cooperative—sometimes they're downright crabby—so you might prefer to string up your curtain with a rope or heavy twine. Outdoors, tie it between two trees, between a building and a tree, or even between two buildings that are the right distance apart. (If you already have a clothesline hanging in the back-yard, use it, and you'll have a curtain that can open and close like a real stage.) Indoors, hang the curtain from drapery rods or from the top of tall

Getting the Show on the Road   127

FIGURE 16

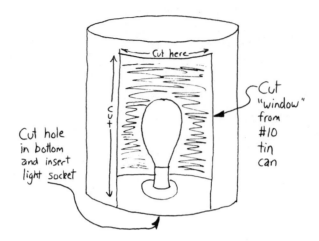

Cut here

Cut

Cut "window" from #10 tin can

Cut hole in bottom and insert light socket

pieces of furniture. Another good place to hang it is in the doorway or arch between two rooms.

For the curtain itself, use an old bedsheet, a blanket, or even a shower curtain, fastening it to the rope with snap-type clothespins (which will let the curtain slide), with large blanket or diaper pins, or with shower curtain hooks (Figure 18).

FIGURE 17

Putting on a Play

FIGURE 18

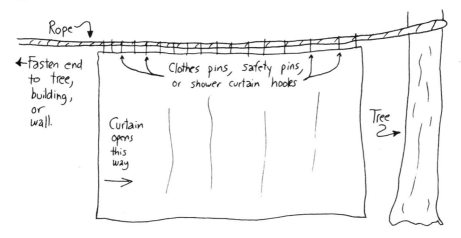

Sets and Props. These two terms are short words for longer ones: the **setting** of a play (meaning the location where it happens) and its **properties** (the various gizmos and gadgets—from frying pans to baseball bats— that are called for in the script). We've already told you about painted backdrops and scenery for the set of your play, so in this section will concentrate on *movable* parts of the set such as the furniture and the collection of properties you'll need to make the play a success.

You have a range of choices available to you, depending on how much time the director and producer want to spend on this part of the production. At one extreme, you can put on a play with strictly imaginary sets and props, either telling the audience what to imagine or giving them clues through pantomime. As we've said before, this kind of theater requires careful concentration on the part of the actors, and it keeps attention focused on *them* rather than on the beauties of the set. If you choose to go this route, the director should work very closely with the actors and actresses so they make the play seem believable. The players should remember where all the furniture is supposed to be and where the doors and windows are, so someone doesn't seem to walk over a studio couch or through a supposedly solid wall. Similarly, the actors and actresses should

Getting the Show on the Road   **129**

practice miming various actions so they seem real—spread the imaginary peanut butter on an imaginary piece of bread, not directly on your hand; place the imaginary glass on an imaginary table when you're through drinking from it rather than drinking and leaving it hanging in midair.

At the other extreme, you might want to make your sets and props complete in every detail and as true to life as you can make them. If this is the case, the producer might want to get the assistance of a **stage manager** and/or a **property master** to keep track of all the things you will accumulate. To go this route, you'll need to do a lot of scrounging in your and your friends' houses, borrowing and collecting furniture and props that will be returned later. If the script calls for the heroine to tease her hair with an eggbeater, you'll need one. If the hero is to have his slippers brought in by the dog, you'll need a pair of slippers (and a dog). Attention to detail is important with this kind of setting. If your play is supposed to take place one hundred years ago, you can't use a chrome-and-glass cocktail table that looks as if it belongs in a science-fiction play. You'll need to search for items that seem authentic for the period or the place you are trying to portray.

In the end, we'd guess that you'll want to settle for something in the middle: sets and props that cover all the "basics" but leave some parts to the imagination of the audience. For instance, if your characters are to have a long conversation on the deck of a ship, you might want to locate deck chairs or lawn furniture for them to sit on, but you probably won't need to locate a rubber raft to serve as a lifeboat. (Or, if you're using flats, you might simply paint on the boat.) A discussion among the director, producer, stage manager, property manager, and the rest of the cast may be useful in deciding just how detailed you want to make your sets and props.

Remember, too, that all that stuff will have to be moved on and off stage during the actual production. (If you forget, the stage manager, dripping with perspiration from the effort of moving it, will remind you.) Sometimes neighborhood theater plays consist of a number of short scenes taking place in different locations. If you use elaborate sets, you'll need long intermissions between scenes, and that, in turn, can make an audience grow restless, in addition to tiring out your stage crew.

Above all, the producer should make certain that the various properties are all *there* for the final production and are organized to be gotten on and off stage effectively. Nothing can be more embarrassing or worrisome than for the heroine to reach for a letter she's supposed to read and find that it is not on the table after all, or for the hero to go to the closet for his rifle and discover that it's missing. The person managing all these objects should prepare a long list indicating what is needed on stage when, and the director of the show should make a set of notes in the margin of his or her script to serve as a duplicate. Then the various props and furniture pieces can be lined up offstage in the order they are needed, and members of the stage crew can take responsibility for getting them on stage. Some theater troupes even hold a separate set of rehearsals for the stage crew, having them practice changing the set until it goes smoothly.

Costumes. Costuming a play can become quite complicated, so much so that you may want to add a **wardrobe master** or **mistress** to your production crew, someone to take charge of finding or making appropriate costumes and seeing they get on the right players at the right time during the course of the play. You don't need to become too elaborate with costuming, however, and it can sometimes be a mistake to try to deck out each actor or actress in a complete and authentic costume for his or her part.

We suggest that you try something called *symbolic costumes*, which simply means that you try to find *one* costume item for each character that will reveal his or her role in the play. For example, an astronaut can wear a motorcycle helmet with a visor to show his/her work. A lady in high society might be represented simply by a tiara (made from an ordinary headband to which you have glued some glitter) and her gentleman by a top hat. An explorer in the jungle can wear a pith helmet (a jungle hat) to show his role; an investigative reporter might carry a notebook around to show her function.

If you are planning to continue writing and producing plays, you and your friends might want to start a costume box or costume trunk to build up a supply of costumes. Save old dresses and trousers, shoes and shirts, hats and coats—items that have outlived their usefulness and are about to be thrown away. Fold them neatly and put them in the costume trunk for possible later use. Then when you're ready to put on a play, open up the trunk and you may be surprised that you can outfit most of your cast from what you already have on hand. (Costume boxes are also fun for rainy-day activities; simply open the box, pick out a costume, and roleplay whatever the costume seems to suggest.)

Costumes can also be made from scratch—designed specially for your play and sewn to order, probably with the help of someone's parent who is good at sewing. Homemade costumes *are* nice to have, but they are rather expensive and time consuming, probably best saved for special occasions or especially important plays.

However, there is an inexpensive way of making simple costumes that you may find helpful—it's called the *basic tunic*, and it's a garment you can slip over your head and tie at the waist. A tunic can be made out of inexpensive cloth—old bedsheets work well—colored or plain, and it can be decorated any number of ways to create a costume for a character. To make one (or, better, make a whole batch of tunics at once) cut a piece of cloth about 18 inches wide and 48 inches long. In the center, cut an oval or circle about 8 inches in diameter for the head. Then get someone in your family who sews to *hem* the edges of the cloth so they won't unravel (Figure 19). To wear the tunic, simply slip it over your head and fasten it around the waist with a belt, ribbon, or piece of string.

Then decorate the tunic. For example, you can:

- Glue patches or pieces of cloth to represent pockets, badges, stripes and decorations, symbols or emblems.
- Draw on it, using permanent felt-tip pens to indicate what the costume is supposed to represent.

FIGURE 19

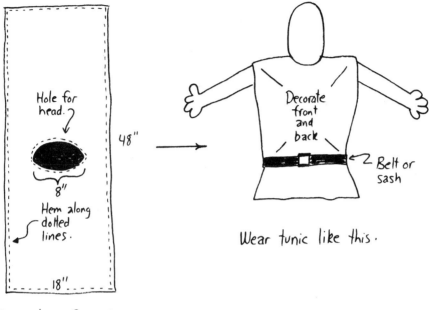

Hole for head.

48"

8"

Hem along dotted lines.

18"

Decorate front and back

Belt or sash

Wear tunic like this.

Make tunic from plain or colored cloth.

- Pin things on it.
- Dye it a different color.

Some examples of how you can turn your plain tunic into a costume are shown in Figure 20. (Note: If making tunics seems too time-consuming or too expensive, you can use most of the same decorating techniques on a plain white T-shirt to get similar effects.)

Makeup. Fancy costumes will never cover up a bad job of acting, nor will a clever use of makeup. If your actors and actresses are to be convincing, they must do it through their own words and actions, not relying on cover-ups. Like costuming, makeup can enhance your performance, mak-

Getting the Show on the Road   133

ROMAN

Plain tunic with strip of sheet for belt.

FOOTBALL PLAYER

Felt letters and numbers.

"KILLER" 86

Dye tunic in team color.

THE DRAGON

Dye tunic green.

Draw scales with felt-tip pen.

(Side View)

Glue felt or paper "spines" on back.

ASTRONAUT

YOU KNOW WHO

S

(Wear tunic over mild-mannered costume.)

SHERIFF

Bandanna

Cut tunic from checked cloth.

Sew or glue on pocket.

Pinned on badge

Fancy western buckle

SOCIALITE

Fake pearls

Tie-dye tunic an elegant color.

Sash made of ribbon

FIGURE 20

ing the players seem to be more like what they're supposed to be. But it's no substitute for a well-rehearsed play.

The art of makeup in the theater and for the films is a book in itself, and it you're deeply interested, you should go to the library and find a book on the subject. In addition, at theater supply stores you can find elegant and expensive makeup kits with greasepaint, strips of false hair, and flesh-colored putty for making puffy noses and cheeks. You can invest time and money in that sort of kit if you want, but we suggest that for neighborhood theater you can find most of what you need to do a good makeup job right around home, usually in a bathroom cabinet.

But before you begin scrounging around to create your own makeup kit, talk to your parents and get permission. The girls reading this book already know how angry mothers and older sisters can get if a new lipstick or a new container of blush has been opened and wrecked. Guys: Don't find out. Don't use somebody else's makeup without permission. Ask a woman to give you her makeup "leftovers"—a lipstick that is worn down to the last quarter inch, a box of powder in a shade she no longer uses. If you and the members of your cast will ask around, you can build a wonderful makeup kit from just these leftovers.

Some things to look for around the bathroom:

Liquid Makeup. This comes in many different shades. Use it all over the players' faces to create a darker skin tone that will look natural under the lights.

Face Powder. White powder is terrific for creating ghosts. (Mimes frequently go in whiteface, too.) It can also be combed or dusted through your hair to make it look gray. Other tones of face powder can be used just like liquid makeup. For really wierd faces like blue or green or purple, get some colored chalk, grind it to a powder, and mix it with basic white powder.

Rouge or Blush. This usually comes in cakes and has a slightly greasy feel to it. For women's makeup it is touched on the cheeks to create a blush.

In the theater you can use it the same way, putting on more than the usual amount to make your characters look flushed and healthy under the lights.

Eye Shadow. This stuff is ordinarily used on the eyelids to create a glamorous effect, and it comes in a number of interesting shades and colors, including blue, green, purple, and grey. Try using it *under* your eyes to create an effect of "hollow" or tired eyes. Rub some on your cheeks to create a hollow effect there—the "death's head" look of a phantom or spirit. If you are creating Frankenstein's monster, rub green lightly all over its face; purple goes well on outer-space critters.

Eye Pencil. This is ordinarily used to create highlights around a woman's eyes, but in the theater is best for creating wrinkles. Draw some "crow's feet" at the corner of your eyes and watch yourself age fifteen years. Draw a bunch of wrinkles on your face and presto, you've aged another twenty years. Eye pencil can also be used to create scars and other markings on the face.

Lipstick. Most actresses and actors wear a little lipstick on stage so their lips won't "fade out" under the lights. Experiment with that, but also look for odd shades of lipstick—purple, pink, magenta, plum—and see how that can be used on your cheeks to create interesting effects.

Remover. Don't leave this off your shopping list. After the play is over, have on hand some makeup *remover* so you can get the stuff off your face.

Fake Nails. These can be glued over your regular nails to create fantastically long and even grotesque nails for certain characters. (Caution: These have to be cut or filed off later; they don't just slip off your fingers.)

Fake Eyelashes. Good to use for your especially "feminine" heroine so she can bat them at boyfriends.

Wigs and Hairpieces. Again, ask permission before you use these.

Cotton. Left white, it can be stuck on a boy's face to create an old man's eyebrows and mustache. It can also be dyed with ink or liquid shoe polish to create a darker-haired person.

And so on . . . turn your imagination loose with the materials you find and you can figure out all sorts of interesting things to do with makeup.

Make certain you practice putting on the makeup at least once before the show goes on so you can get the effects you want. Also leave plenty of time to apply it on the actual night of the performance.

Advertising Your Play

Even as your play goes into rehearsal, you should be thinking about attracting an audience to see it. Of course, your parents, family, and close friends will probably come anyway, but given the amount of work that goes into the production of many plays, you should think about attracting a larger audience from your neighborhood and possibly from your entire community. Because people's lives are very busy in our modern society, with many commitments to be "someplace else," attracting a crowd to a play is not always easy, and your advertising campaign will require careful planning and precise execution. You may even want to have an advertising manager to take responsibility for it, though for a small play the producer and the cast may be able to handle it by themselves.

For many neighborhood theater productions, *word-of-mouth* advertising may be enough to draw a crowd. Tell your cast members to begin talking up the play, telling their friends and neighbors about it. They should tell a little about what will happen in the play (without giving away the plot) and describe the cast. In making a sales pitch, stress that the play is written, produced, and acted by kids, that this is not simply a production of an adult-written play. You'll find that will increase people's interest in your work. Your ad manager can leave word-of-mouth advertising on an informal basis, but it can also be organized into a *door-to-door* canvass on an agreed-upon date. That way, he or she can split your neighborhood into sections and guarantee that all possible viewers have heard about the play. Be certain to instruct your canvassers to tell people the date, place, and time of the play, and urge people to write it down on their calendars.

But people often forget, so you might want to enhance your word-of-mouth campaign with some *brochures* or *fliers* about the play. These can

FIGURE 21

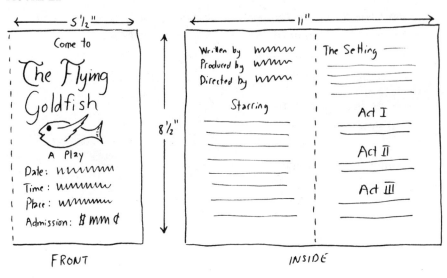

be duplicated on a mimeograph or spirit duplicator (ask your school or church secretary about that) or taken to a commercial copy shop to be printed at low cost. One good way to do a brochure is shown in Figure 21, using a standard-sized 8½ × 11 inch piece of paper. On the front page print an ad for the play; on the inside, print an actual copy of the program with the names of the cast and a summary of the main acts. This brochure is effective because it tells possible audience members exactly what the play will be about and when it will take place. Deliver your brochures or fliers to every house and apartment in your neighborhood. Ask permission of local storeowners to leave a few copies by the checkout counter near the cash register.

If brochures seem too complicated or are too expensive for your budget, consider making some *posters* to advertise the play. You can make these from sheets of brightly colored poster board, from construction paper, or from the sides of a cardboard box, painted in a bright color. Make certain your poster contains the vital information:

WHAT? (*The title of the play*)
WHO? (*The names of the players, author, director, producer*)
WHERE? (*The location of the theater*)
WHEN? (*The date and time*)
HOW MUCH? (*The admission charge, if there is one*)

Posters can be placed in the hallways at school, in the windows of neighborhood stores and restaurants, and on announcement or bulletin boards at shopping centers and malls. But before you put a poster anyplace, check with somebody in charge to get permission. Often there are regulations about posting advertisements, even for worthy activities like your play.

Radio, television, and *newspaper* advertising can be free—put away your checkbook—if you know how to go about it. Most newspapers run announcements of community events on a regular basis, and radio and television stations are required by law to give a certain amount of their broadcast day to public-service announcements. To get your announcement on the air or in print, first prepare a clear and legible copy of your announcement, typed if possible. Give the basic who-what-when-where-how much information as clearly and *briefly* as you can, remembering that newspaper space and air time are valuable and must be used efficiently. Then stick copies of your announcement in envelopes, mark them "Attention: Community Service Announcements," and address them to various local television and radio stations and newspapers. (You can get a full list of these by consulting the yellow or white pages and looking under *Newspapers* and *Broadcasting Companies* or *Radio* and *Television Broadcasting Companies.*)

One warning about media advertising: It can be very effective, reaching hundreds of thousands of people. Before you decide to send your announcement to the media, make certain you can handle the crowd that might come. If your play is being held in a school or church auditorium, you will probably be able to seat as many people as might be attracted by your announcement. But if the play is being given in somebody's basement or backyard, media advertising might get you a larger audience than you can provide seating for.

Curtain Up!

This is it. The rehearsals are over and done with. Your advertising campaign is complete and you know that a good crowd will be in attendance. It's time to get on with the show.

In the excitement of putting on the play—getting actors and actresses into costume and makeup, curing a nervous actor or actress of those what-if-I-forget-my-lines worries—it's possible for a theater company to overlook some important details.

For example, you will need to assign somebody to *prepare the theater* beforehand. If your play is being given in a basement or backyard, somebody needs to take responsibility to get enough chairs to seat your anticipated audience and to arrange the chairs the way you want them. If the play will be given at a school or church, it may be necessary to have someone arrive early to have the janitor unlock the doors and turn on the lights. In addition, the people in charge of properties and wardrobe will need to arrive early to organize the materials they will be needing. (It's also a good idea to have the actors and actresses arrive well in advance, just to save yourself nervous worry about whether or not a key player will be there for the performance.)

You will probably need someone to *sell* and/or *collect tickets* for the program. Are you going to charge admission? If you are, the price should be set low enough that people—especially other kids—are not kept away because of the price. At the same time, it would be nice if your show made a modest amount to cover any expenses you had in putting it on and perhaps to pay for a small cast party afterward.

You'll probably need some *ushers* to escort people to their seats. The ushers usually give out *programs*, printed beforehand, telling people about the play, the players, and the author, director, producer, and stage crew.

Having *refreshments* available is another tradition in the theater and an opportunity for you to make a dollar or two. You might assign a younger brother or sister to this task, somebody who's had experience running a summer lemonade stand. Refreshments might consist of popcorn (that's cheap and easy to make) and some sort of punch or fruit juice that can be made up in quantity. The person running the refreshment stand will also need to remember paper cups and other supplies. And someone will need to be assigned the task of cleaning up the theater afterward, not just the empty cups and popcorn bags, but the discarded programs as well.

And then . . . it's all over. The play has been given, the audience enjoyed it, and the stage is dark. Then it's time to celebrate with the cast party, including everybody who helped in producing the play and getting it staged. The cast party is the time to talk about how the show went, to remember highlights, to laugh (not cry) about muffed lines or missed entrances, to recapture some of the high points and generally bask in the glow of success. It's also a good time to chow down some ice cream and cake—the cast will be starved after the show, and the director will be able to eat for the first time in days.

Organizing Your Own Theater Company

At your cast party, somebody will probably say:

"This was fun. I'm sorry it's over."

or

"Let's do this again, soon."

That can be your cue that what's needed in your neighborhood is a theater *company:* a group of showpeople—actors and actresses, producers and stagehands, writers and directors—who can put on plays regularly. Certainly, after all the effort you've put into just one presentation, it seems worthwhile considering taking the show on the road to present to other audiences.

If you look around your community and ask, you can probably find a number of places where you can put on your plays, including:

Schools—Your English, language arts, or drama teacher might like to have you put on the play for his/her class, or maybe even for the whole school. Another possibility worth investigating is taking the play to a class of younger children, who will be delighted to see a play put on by big kids.

Parks—Many park districts have cultural and recreational programs, especially in the summertime. Find out the name of the park district director and phone or write, asking about the possibility of putting on your play there.

Homes for the Elderly—The elderly and shut-ins often enjoy having young people around, and they will make an extremely appreciative audience for your play. Ask your parents to help you make contact with the appropriate people.

Hospitals—The children's ward is an especially good place to put on a play, but you might be able to do a performance for hospitalized adults as well.

Fairs and *Celebrations*—Many communities have street fairs and special events that are celebrated each year, often with entertainment provided. If your community has such events, call up City Hall and ask about ways in which your theater company can become involved.

Malls and *Shopping Centers*—These places are constantly on the lookout for special events that range from dog shows to displays of antique cars as a way of attracting shoppers. Contact the manager of the mall and ask if your neighborhood theater troupe can put on a show.

Taking the show on the road this way is not quite the same as doing it in your own backyard. You may have to make the sets and props simpler, and sometimes you will be putting on a play in the middle of a room, with no formal stage at all. With a little practice, however, you and your players can become quite skilled at presenting your drama in a new or unfamiliar location. You can even learn how to get the props you need into a few boxes or trunks so that you can move into and out of a new location easily.

We hope that this book has helped you—maybe even inspired you—to create and produce a play or two of your own. If you enjoyed that process, forming your own neighborhood theater company will give you the chance to enjoy creating a theatrical production . . . again, and again, and again.

A Glossary
of Stage Terms

Auditions. (See **Casting**)

Call Boy or **Call Girl.** A person who works offstage, keeping track of when actors and actresses make their entrances and notifying them so they are ready on time.

Casting. Finding players to fit the various parts and characters in a play. If a director has more actors and actresses than parts, he or she may want to hold auditions, where players read a section of the script to show their acting skills.

Center Stage. (See **Stage**)

Character. An imaginary person or animal written into a play by the author. In another sense, *character* is also the quality of personality or pizzazz that the imaginary characters have. Your characters must have *character*.

Climax. The high point of a play, the moment when the problem or **conflict** is at its absolute peak. Usually after the climax a play moves directly to its ending or conclusion. Sometimes, though, the climax *is* the end of the play, with the problem or conflict resolved only at the last possible moment.

Conflict. The struggle or problem that makes a play move. A conflict may be between two people, among several people, or between a person and some problem that he or she faces. When the conflict comes to an end (either happily or sadly for the characters) the play also comes to an end.

Dialogue. The words or lines spoken by the actors and actresses in a play. Good, rapid-moving dialogue is essential to having an interesting play, and realistic dialogue (speeches that sound as if real people made them) makes a play come to life for the audience.

Dramatic Monologue. One person talking by himself or herself on stage. Sometimes the player giving a dramatic monologue will appear to be talking to the audience, filling them in on what is happening in the play. At other times, the player talks to himself or herself aloud, letting the audience listen in on "private" thoughts.

Director. The person responsible for organizing the actors and actresses and coaching them in the presentation of a play. In neighborhood theater, the director will often be the person who wrote the play.

Dress Rehearsal. (See **Rehearsal**)

Downstage. (See **Stage**)

Flat. A standing piece of wood or cardboard painted with scenery or serving as a wall of a room.

Improvisation/Improvised Drama. A play made up by the actors and actresses as they go along, with little or no preparation and with no script to guide them.

Media/Media Plays. Radio drama, television plays, and films—any method for "storing" a play on tape or film for presentation to an audience later.

Mime. (See **Pantomime**)

Narrator. A person—part of the play—who explains to the audience what is happening or is about to happen. Frequently the narration will be presented as a **dramatic monologue.** A narrator is used most often in radio plays, where the audience cannot see the "set" and needs to be given some basic background information.

Pantomime. A play without words. In pantomime (or **mime**) the players rely entirely on gestures to make their meaning clear.

Plot. The story line of a play—what the play is all about. Usually the plot will center on a **conflict** among the characters or a problem which they must overcome. The plot becomes more and more complicated until it reaches a **climax,** and the problem arrives at a **resolution** or solution.

Producer. The person who handles the details of production of a play, helping the director organize rehearsals, taking charge of the stage crew, even planning for the advertising of the play.

Prompter. A person who works offstage, following the script, and helping players who have forgotten their lines by whispering (a stage whisper) to them enough words to get them going again.

Proscenium Arch. (See **Stage**)

Property/Prop. The various objects that are used as part of a play production, ranging from big things like pieces of furniture to small things like pins or matches or handkerchiefs.

Property Mistress or **Master.** A member of the stage crew whose sole responsibility is keeping track of the props, making certain they are organized and on stage when needed.

Reader's Theater. A play presented by actors and actresses who read a script aloud but do not memorize it or develop any gestures to go with it. A radio play is one example of reader's theater, with the final product recorded on tape. But reader's theater can be presented before a live audience as well.

Rehearsal. Practice. Rehearsals usually begin with a simple oral reading of a script, then a more formal **reader's theater** reading in which the players try to get life into their roles. A **walk-through** comes next, with the players (either reading scripts or having memorized their lines) going through the play slowly, figuring out where they will stand on stage, how they will get on and off stage, and so on. The final practice session is usually a **dress rehearsal** in full costume, with no stops or breaks, the play being presented just as it would be for a real audience.

Repertory Company. A group of players, stagehands, a director, producer, and playwright who travel about putting on plays. The collection of plays which they can do is called their **repertoire.**

Resolution. The moment in a play when the central **conflict** or problem is solved.

Script. The written-out version of a play, containing not only lines for the players, but directions for the stage crew, property master/mistress, and even filmmakers or video technicians if they are involved in the play.

Setting/Set. The place where a play takes place. In one sense, the **setting** is an imaginary place, described by the author in the stage directions. The **set** is the literal place where the play happens, a place with flats and props and scenery that represents the setting for the audience.

Skit. Almost any kind of play, but usually used to describe informal presentations done without elaborate planning beforehand. Often **improvised drama.**

Stage. The place where the play takes place. It can be a spot where an audience imagines the setting to be, or it can be a formal stage such as in a theater or auditorium. The basic parts of the stage include the **proscenium arch** (the frame for the stage made by the curtains), various **flats** to serve as walls or scenery, and the stage platform itself. The locations on stage are referred to as **center stage** (the middle), **stage right** and **left** (the right and left side as seen by an actor facing the audience), **upstage** (toward the back), and **downstage** (toward the audience).

Stage Directions. Instructions for performance written into the script, including a description of the setting, directions for the actors and actresses, descriptions of sound effects, and so on.

Stage Hands or **Stage Crew.** The people who supply the muscle of handling arrangements on and offstage, moving sets and props, pulling curtains, handling the lights, and doing the sound effects. In neighborhood theater, the stage crew may often be the players themselves.

Stage Manager. A person assigned by the producer to be boss of the **stage crew** and responsible for offstage arrangements.

Understudy. A person who learns one or several roles for the play and is ready to step in if an actor or actress is unable to appear.

Upstage. A location on the stage toward the back. (See also **stage.**) Also a term used to describe an actor or actress who tries to make himself or herself the center of attention on stage. To "upstage" a fellow player, an actor or actress would walk to the back of the stage (upstage), forcing the other players to turn their backs to the audience and muffling their lines.

Walk-through. (See **Rehearsal**)

Wardrobe Master or **Mistress.** The person in charge of costumes for a play.

Index